Socrates Meets Sartre

Other Works of Peter Kreeft from St. Augustine's Press

Philosophy 101 by Socrates
Socrates Meets Descartes
Socrates Meets Freud
Socrates Meets Hume
Socrates Meets Kant
Socrates Meets Kierkegaard
Socrates Meets Machiavelli
Socrates Meets Marx
The Philosophy of Jesus
Jesus-Shock
Summa Philosophica
Socratic Logic
Socrates' Children: Ancient
Socrates' Children: Medieval
Socrates' Children: Modern
Socrates' Children: Contemporary
Socrates' Children [all four books in one]
An Ocean Full of Angels
The Sea Within
I Surf, Therefore I Am
If Einstein Had Been a Surfer

Socrates Meets Sartre

The Father of Philosophy Cross-Examines
the Founder of Existentialism

A Socratic Dialogue on
Existentialism and Human Emotion

By Peter Kreeft

ST. AUGUSTINE'S PRESS
South Bend, Indiana

Manufactured in the United States of America

1 2 3 4 5 6   20 19 18 17 16 15 14

Library of Congress Control Number: 2020935698

✕ The paper used in this publication meets the minimum requirements of
the American National Standard for Information Sciences Permanence of
Paper for Printed Materials, ANSI Z39.481984.

St. Augustine's Press
www.staugustine.net

Contents

Introduction

This book is one in a series of Socratic explorations of some of the Great Books. Books in this series are intended to be short, clear, and non-technical, thus fully understandable by beginners. They also introduce (or review) the basic questions in the fundamental divisions of philosophy (see the chapter titles): metaphysics, epistemology, anthropology, ethics, logic, and method. They are designed both for classroom use and for educational do-it-yourselfers. The "Socrates Meets . . ." books can be read and understood completely on their own, but each is best appreciated after reading the little classic it engages in dialogue.

The setting—Socrates and the author of the Great Book meeting in the afterlife—need not deter readers who do not believe there is an afterlife. For although the two characters and their philosophies are historically real, their conversation, of course, is not and requires a "willing suspension of disbelief". There is no reason the skeptic cannot extend this literary belief also to the setting.

I

In Hell?

SARTRE: Oh, the absurdity of it all! The absurdity! The absurdity! That I exist! Even after I have died, I still exist! How utterly nauseating! It is indeed the nausea of existence itself. There is indeed "no exit" from my own existence! I am in Hell, forever!

SOCRATES (to himself): He whines like a sick puppy. He pouts and preens like a bratty teenager. He drowns in the lake of his own verbosity like Narcissus. And yet this man is called a philosopher, a lover of wisdom. He was more popular in his lifetime than any other in his century. (What a century!) Thousands of adoring women flung themselves at him to be abused. I have been here in the Overworld for nearly twenty-four centuries, examining mankind, as part of their Purgatory and my Heaven, but sometimes I think I shall never understand human nature.

Well, there is mystery here, at any rate: that much is clear. Perhaps I can learn as well as teach in this encounter. But I may have to abandon my "Socratic method" for stronger medicines, if I am to get through to this patient. For this conversation, so that he can relate to me, I shall speak like an ordinary philosopher, not like myself. He does not see or hear me yet—or anything or anyone else, for that matter.

SARTRE: Alas, alas, the absurdity of it all, the absurdity of my existence!

SOCRATES: He is indeed in absurdity, but not because of his existence.

SARTRE: It is as I thought: my very being is a **"being-for-itself"**, endlessly frustrated in its inescapable and unending attempt to do the impossible, to become a **"being-in-itself"**. But there is **"no exit"** from this self-contradiction. My own noblest possession, freedom, is my doom: I am **"condemned to freedom."** I am doomed to failure. I am an eternal Boston Red Sox fan, under a cosmic curse.

SOCRATES: He attempts to drown himself and his misery in the ocean of his own verbiage. He is right: *that* attempt is doomed to failure.

SARTRE: But am I really in Hell? How can that be? **"Hell is other people."** But I see no other people here, either my torturers or my torturees.

SOCRATES: That is because your ugly eyeballs are ingrown, like toenails, Jean-Paul. Look outside yourself for once! Look here! Look at me!

SARTRE: Oh, oh. I spoke too soon. Here comes my torturer. O cruel and cursed irony of the gods—my torturer is to be Socrates! Objective truth in a toga!

SOCRATES: It could be worse, Jean-Paul; it could have been Jesus.

SARTRE: No, no, there are no "could have beens." There are no possibilities, there are only actualities.

SOCRATES: Not so. You could have been Jean-Paul the Great. But that name will be given to another, with whom you will never be confused. You are Jean-Paul the Small.

SARTRE: I do not answer to that name.

SOCRATES: But it answers to you. It hovers round your head like a halo.

SARTRE: A halo, you say?

SOCRATES: A tiny, dark halo.

SARTRE: I accept my fate: to be tortured, to be insulted, to be known by you as an object, a being-in-itself. But where is *my* victim? Each torturee must be a torturer as well.

SOCRATES: Not so. That pattern was broken when One became the universal torturee.

SARTRE: Not so. He is the torturer. He would be my torturer if He were present to me now.

SOCRATES: Perhaps that is why He is not present.

SARTRE: He lets you do His dirty work, then, Socrates?

SOCRATES: My work is only to explore and examine *your work*.

SARTRE: What work?

SOCRATES: Your best book.

SARTRE: All 700 pages of it?

SOCRATES: No, no, not *Saint Genet*. That was your *worst* book: as perverse as DeSade but infinitely duller. I mean *Existentialism and Human Emotions*.

SARTRE: But that was my *shortest* book.

SOCRATES: Precisely. And that is why it was so precise and intelligible.

SARTRE: But most of it was culled from *Being and Nothingness*.

SOCRATES: Yes. A good panhandler can find a few nuggets of gold even in a river of mud.

SARTRE: I can endure your Socratic questioning, and even your sarcastic personal insults, if you only answer me one little question.

SOCRATES: "Just answer me one little question"— that's *my* line. I am flattered by your plagiarism. And also curious about your question. What is it?

SARTRE: Well, as you know, I didn't believe in Hell or Heaven or Purgatory or any sort of life after death. It seems I was wrong about life after death; was I wrong about Hell too? In *No Exit* I used it as a metaphor for earth, for how we always inescapably deal with each other in life. Thus **"Hell is other people."** Am I now in my own play? Is that to be my punishment?

SOCRATES: You said you had one question. By my count that's three.

SARTRE: Am I in Hell or not?

SOCRATES: That is entirely up to you.

SARTRE: Look here, Socrates, if that is really who you are, could you give me just one little gift? Could you use another instrument of torture than your famous "Socratic method"? I mean those teasing questions of yours, and then those long, repetitious, and insultingly elementary chains of logic that you are so in love with. Could you instead come right to the point? Just hit me, already. It will make me less cranky than your intellectual version of Chinese water torture, and *whatever* you want from me, you'll get more out of me if I'm less cranky.

SOCRATES: I promise I will try to be quick. Quicker than you were in most of your books, at any rate.

2

The First Principle
of Existentialism

SARTRE: I promised to endure your questioning and you promised to try to be quick. So let's get on with it. Where do we begin?

SOCRATES: If we are to examine your philosophy, we need an approach, a method, a sort of road map first, don't you agree? For your philosophy is like a fugue: every major theme is connected with every other one. So we could enter this unified structure from any point and be led to all the others. Your thought is like a work of art: unified and consistent in itself.

SARTRE: Thank you for understanding that. And—?

SOCRATES: What do you mean "And—"?

SARTRE: I mean, What's the catch?

SOCRATES: Catch? There is no catch. I just gave you a compliment; why is it easier for you to accept an insult than a compliment?

SARTRE: Is that another insult? Or would you really like me to answer that question?

SOCRATES: I *would* really like that, because I think that thereby hangs a tale. But not now. It would be much more comprehensible later, when we understand your first principles.

SARTRE: Why not now? You admitted that one can enter my philosophy at any point. Why not here, then, with a phenomenology of compliments and insults? That would be a nicely concrete starting point.

SOCRATES: I think we should follow the traditional order from the more abstract and general principles to the more concrete and particular applications, for the sake of clarity, and brevity, and to avoid repeating ourselves and going round in circles.

SARTRE: I prefer the opposite order.

SOCRATES: I know you do. But the traditional order is clearer: first metaphysics—"What is?"—then anthropology—"What am I?"—then ethics—"What should I do?"

SARTRE: Order doesn't really matter. Inquire away.

SOCRATES: Let us begin at the beginning: *your* beginning, your title and your explanation of it at the beginning of your book. You coined the term "existentialism", didn't you?

SARTRE: No, the media did. In 1944, when they asked me to define the term, I answered, "I don't know what it is." But I decided to plagiarize from those plagiarizers, so I adopted it. In 1945, I entitled my famous public lecture "Existentialism as a Humanism". They were agog, and I felt like a god instead of a frog with goggles, which is what I look like. But—what am I saying? I just called myself a frog! Why am I compelled to tell the truth here?

This never happened to me on earth. What is the cause of this intolerable constraint?

SOCRATES: You are not ready to know that now.

SARTRE: I have lost my freedom! I have lost my humanity! I am in Hell!

SOCRATES: You have lost your freedom to lie. You have not lost your humanity; you are being given a chance to grasp it and confront it. And where you are is in your own power, your own choice.

SARTRE: I understand only your third point.

SOCRATES: I think you do not understand that at all. And I think you do understand the other two. But no more diversions! We must get on with our task of examining your book.

SARTRE: How can my "I" be a diversion from my book? Isn't it the other way round?

SOCRATES: Yes indeed. But we must begin with the easier examination. The harder one will come later, and it will require powers much greater than mine.

SARTRE: I am afraid.

SOCRATES: That is the most sensible thing you have said yet. Perhaps there is hope for you after all.

SARTRE: I am far more comfortable with despair than with hope.

SOCRATES: I know. You are truly a twisted soul.

SARTRE: Why, thank you very much!

SOCRATES: But a brilliant one, nevertheless.

SARTRE: Damn you, Socrates, you really know how to torture a man!

SOCRATES: And you really know how to divert one. But not here. We must examine your book now.

SARTRE: I hate that word "must".

SOCRATES: So what?

SARTRE: Do my feelings not count here?

SOCRATES: Of course not! We both have far more important things to focus on.

SARTRE: Do you claim that my words are more important than my feelings?

SOCRATES: Did you entitle your autobiography *The Feelings*?

SARTRE: No.

SOCRATES: What title did you choose?

SARTRE: *The Words*.

SOCRATES: And you shall have what you chose. In the end, all get what they want.

SARTRE: That is not believable.

SOCRATES: It is, if only you distinguish what you really want from what you think you want, and also from what you feel. You *know* what you think and what you feel, and it is easy to put that into words, especially for one with your intellectual and verbal powers. But what you really want—that is darker and deeper, and it requires delicate and indirect handling to explore it. Our job here is only to explore your words. So let us finally begin—with your title and the title of your whole philosophy in one word: "Existentialism". What, essentially, does it mean?

SARTRE: As I explained in the book, it means that **"existence precedes essence."**

SOCRATES: That sounds like a formula from the metaphysics of St. Thomas Aquinas.

SARTRE: It is metaphysical, but it is certainly not Thomistic. It is not what he might mean by it, namely an analysis of the metaphysical structure of all finite beings, culminating in the claim that existence is the supreme actuality and that essence is only the potentiality to exist. Rather, in my philosophy it is an analysis of the mode of being unique to man, or to any conscious subject.

SOCRATES: You were very adept at manipulating abstract concepts like that. But you were also very adept at illustrating them with concrete images and analogies that were unforgettable. Such as the paper cutter. Could you read that passage from your book?

SARTRE: Where is my book? Aha! Here it is, in my hands as soon as I want it. Is this the place you get everything you desire?

SOCRATES: No, that place is called Hell. This is only Purgatory.

SARTRE: I don't know whether you are joking or serious.

SOCRATES: Serious, I assure you.

SARTRE: But not literal?

SOCRATES: Quite literal. But that is another distraction.

SARTRE: You fear being distracted from your task.

SOCRATES: I fear *your* being distracted from your task. I am here for you, not you for me. So please get on with it. Read the passage.

SARTRE: All right. I'll try to find it—Oh! Here it is. The book opened itself at my will to the very passage I wanted.

"*Existence precedes essence.*" Just what does that mean? Let us consider some object that is manufactured, for example a book or a paper-cutter: here is an object which has been made by an artisan whose inspiration came from a concept. He referred to the concept of what a paper-cutter is and . . . having a specific use; and one can not postulate a man who produces a paper-cutter but does not know what it is used for. Therefore let us say that, for the paper-cutter, essence—that is, the . . . properties which enable it to be both produced and defined—precedes essence.

When we conceive God as the Creator, He is generally thought of as a superior sort of artisan . . . we always grant that will more or less follows understanding, or, at the very least, accompanies it, and that when God creates He knows exactly what He is creating. Thus, the concept of man in the mind of God is comparable to the concept of the

EHE,
13–15

paper-cutter in the mind of the manufac-
turer. . . .

In the eighteenth century, the atheism of
the *philosophes* discarded the idea of God, but
not . . . the notion that essence precedes existence. To a certain extent, this idea is found
everywhere . . . [that] man has a human nature. . . .

Atheistic existentialism, which I represent,
is more coherent. It states that if God does
not exist, there is at least one being in whom
existence precedes essence, a being who exists before he can be defined by any concept, and that this being is man. . . . What
is meant here by saying that existence precedes essence? It means that, first of all, man
exists, turns up, appears on the scene, and
only afterward defines himself. If man, as the
existentialist conceives him, is indefinable, it
is because at first he is nothing. Only afterward will he be something, and he himself
will have made what he will be. Thus, there
is no human nature, since there is no God to
conceive it. . . .

Man is nothing else but what he makes of
himself. Such is the first principle of existentialism.

SOCRATES: Thank you for being so clear and concise.

SARTRE: Are you serious or not? I'm not sure.

SOCRATES: Are you clear and concise or not? I'm not
sure. But you *are* sure that this is your first principle,
are you not?

SARTRE: That man is nothing else but what he makes of himself. Yes. That is my first principle. And it means that man, as the *subject* of consciousness, can have no inherent definable essence like all the *objects* of his consciousness. That is my first principle, and it would be my answer to your famous question "Know thyself."

SOCRATES: And the *reason* you give for this first principle is that **"there is no human nature *since there is no God* to conceive it."**

SARTRE: Yes.

SOCRATES: So you deduce your "first principle", that there is no human nature, from the premise that there is no God.

SARTRE: Yes. That deduction logically follows. But most other atheists do not see that.

SOCRATES: But then it is your *atheism* that is your first principle. The other is your second.

SARTRE: Logically, yes. In terms of importance, no. God is not only unreal but also unimportant to me. At least, His non-existence is far less important than man's existence.

SOCRATES: But you also wrote, later in this book, that **"Existentialism is nothing else than an attempt to draw all the consequences of a coherent atheistic position."**   EHE, 51

SARTRE: I say that too. Those older atheists, the eighteenth century *philosophes*, for instance, were not as logically coherent as I. They did not realize many of the necessary consequences of their atheism. And there are other consequences besides the disappearance of the concept of human nature. For instance, as I said later on in this book, there are logical consequence of atheism in *ethics*:

EHE,
21–22

God does not exist and we have to face all the consequences of this. The existentialist is strongly opposed to a certain kind of secular ethics which would like to abolish God with the least possible expense . . . something like this: God is a useless and costly hypothesis; we are discarding it; but, meanwhile, in order for there to be an ethics, a society, a civilization, it is essential that certain values be taken seriously and that they be considered as having an *a priori* existence. It must be obligatory, *a priori*, to be honest, not to lie, not to beat your wife, to have children, etc., etc. So we're going to try a little device which will make it possible to show that values exist all the same, inscribed in a heaven of ideas, though otherwise God does not exist. We shall find ourselves with the same norms of honesty, progress, and humanism and we shall have made of God an outdated hypothesis which will peacefully die off by itself.

The existentialist, on the contrary, thinks it very distressing that God does not exist, because all possibility of finding values in a heaven of ideas disappears along with Him; there can no longer be an *a priori* Good since

there is no infinite and perfect consciousness to think it. Nowhere is it written that the Good exists, that we must be honest, that we must not lie; because the fact is we are on a plane where there are only men. Dostoyevski said, "If God didn't exist, everything would be possible [permissible]." That is the very starting point of existentialism. Indeed, everything is permissible if God does not exist, and as a result man is forlorn, because neither within him nor without does he find anything to cling to.

SOCRATES: I usually interrupt long speeches to clarify or question each point; but I let you go on, twice now, because both passages are so stunning, so clear, so powerful, and so simple that they almost took my breath away.

SARTRE: Even now, it is impossible to know whether you are serious or ironic.

SOCRATES: I assure you, I am quite serious.

SARTRE: Thank you—I think.

SOCRATES: But you should know that seriousness and irony are not exclusive.

SARTRE: Are you going to torture me with flattery, preachings, or insults?

SOCRATES: I am neither torturer nor flatterer, and I am neither preacher nor insulter.

SARTRE: What are you, then?

SOCRATES: I am a mirror. I am a light. I am a question. My only sermon is "Know thyself." And to that end I ask this question about your starting point:

Twice you mentioned **"the first principle of existentialism"**, or **"the very starting point of existentialism."** The first was that there is no human essence since there is no God to conceive it and design it. The second thing that you called **"the very starting point of existentialism"** was that everything is permissible since there is no God to conceive and to will the Good for man. These two things are both arguments, and the premise of both arguments is atheism. You deduce two consequences of this premise, first in anthropology (that there is no human nature) and then in ethics (that there is no Good). Have I understood you correctly so far?

SARTRE: Yes. So what is your question?

SOCRATES: Are you a theistic spy planted in the camp of the atheists?

SARTRE: What a ridiculous and insulting thing to say! Why do you say that?

SOCRATES: Because the most likely effect those two passages will have on atheists and agnostics is to send them running into the arms of the nearest priest.

SARTRE: The weaklings, perhaps. Let them go.

SOCRATES: No, I think you have given the *strong* minds two good reasons to reject atheism. You have just strengthened the two most common arguments in the world for the existence of God, I think. Is that what you intended to do?

SARTRE: Of course not. What two arguments are you talking about?

SOCRATES: They are usually called the Design Argument and the Moral Argument. They both take the form of a hypothetical or conditional syllogism, the form logicians call Denying the Consequent. And you have given powerful reasons for accepting the conditional premise of both syllogisms, the one that begins with "If there is no God . . . "

Here, let me state these two arguments. The Design Argument usually argues to God from the design in the cosmos. But it can also argue from the design in man, and then it runs something like this:

- If there is no God who designs man, then man has no design, no "human nature".
- But man obviously does have a human nature.
- Therefore there is a God who designs man.

And the Moral Argument runs like this:

- If God does not exist, then everything is morally permissible.
- But obviously not everything is morally permissible.
- Therefore God exists.

Most people find the *second* premise of each of these two arguments the most obvious one. Thus, most atheists try to avoid the conclusion that God exists by denying the *first* premise, the "if . . . then . . . " one. But you have nailed down the first premise with very heavy nails, in both arguments. So you have probably convinced more people to be theists than atheists.

That is why I asked you whether you were a theist spy.

SARTRE: I am not responsible for fools inverting and subverting and perverting my argument.

SOCRATES: But you said you were.

SARTRE: What? Where?

EHE, 16   SOCRATES: Where you wrote: **"Man is responsible for what he is . . . and . . . we do not only mean that he is responsible for his own individuality, but that he is responsible for all men."**

SARTRE: But that is not what I meant.

SOCRATES: Then why is that what you said?

3

Atheism and Honesty

SOCRATES: Not to say what you mean, or not to mean what you say—is that not what we mean by lying? Oh, now I see. I had forgotten what you said about lying: that since God does not exist, **"nowhere is it written . . . that we must be honest, that we must not lie."** I did not take you seriously when I first read this, but now I see you are quite serious and quite consistent, in your practice as well as your theory: you practice what you preach. You are a logical liar, a consistent liar, an honest liar, a sincere hypocrite. You practice the hypocrisy you preach.

EHE, 22

SARTRE: And you, Socrates: you practice exactly the opposite of what you preach. For you said you do not torture or flatter or preach or insult, and yet you have done all four of these things to me. You are playing with me, and not taking me seriously, as you said you were.

SOCRATES: I am taking you very seriously. I am certainly taking the *question* you raise very seriously. I mean the question about the relation between God and lying, or between God and truth-telling, or between God and truth itself. I think this is one of the most serious questions possible. And I think that you and Nietzsche are the only two philosophers who see clearly how close the relationship is between God and truth, how problematic truth becomes if "God is dead." Nietzsche said that he was raising for the very first time "the most dangerous question", the question about "the will to truth". And the question was shockingly simple and shockingly unanswerable: "Why truth? Why not rather untruth?" Why not "the lie"? It is an absolutely serious question, and it demands an answer. Why not, indeed? Do you have an answer to that question?

SARTRE: We give our answers with our actions, not our words. Or, rather, since writing and speaking are actions, we give our answers in the *act* of writing or speaking, not merely in the *content* of it.

SOCRATES: Do you think that is an answer to Nietzsche's question "Why not untruth?"

SARTRE: It is *my* answer.

SOCRATES: Then you must think it is *an* answer. For it must be *an* answer before it can be *your* answer, by the necessary laws of logic.

SARTRE: Not so, Socrates! You presuppose the old way of looking at man: that first he has an essence, and that all his acts follow certain laws, the laws of his essence and of essences in general, such as the laws of logic. I say rather that I *make* my essence by my actions—my actions which constitute my existence, my life. Therefore I say that it is *my* answer *before* it is *an* answer. And it is logically consistent with what I have said earlier.

SOCRATES: But I do not think that most people, if they confront Nietzsche's "most dangerous question", would be satisfied with your answer to it. In fact, I don't think they would even understand it.

SARTRE: You are wrong, Socrates. Many have understood it. *Existentialism and Human Emotions* was one of my simplest books. I didn't even use the most basic technical terminology of my philosophy there. (I mean **"being-in-itself"** and **"being-for-itself."**)

SOCRATES: I think we should have a go at your metaphysical first principle again, using those very categories. But first we should look further into this question of honesty. Even in this simple book, you do give an answer to the question "Why be honest?"

SARTRE: Then what's your problem, Socrates?

SOCRATES: That I do not understand your answer. Here is the passage:

> **Suppose someone says to me, "What if I want to be dishonest?" I'll answer, "There's no reason for you not to be, but I'm saying that that's what you are, and that the strictly coherent attitude is that of honesty."**

EHE, 45

There's no reason for you not to be [dishonest]—well, I suppose that's as clear an answer to the question "Why not be dishonest?" as anyone could ask for. The answer is that there *is* no reason.

SARTRE: So what more do you want?

SOCRATES: To understand the meaning of your answer.

SARTRE: I mean simply that it is your free choice to be honest or dishonest.

SOCRATES: Not *here*, it isn't. Not any more. There is no night here, and no hiding.

SARTRE: On earth, then.

SOCRATES: But that is obvious. No one doubted it. *Of course* it was your free choice to be honest or dishonest; that's why you were responsible for it. My question—Nietzsche's question—is a different one: *Why* be honest?

SARTRE: Because you have chosen to, and that is your being, that's what you are. You are your choices.

SOCRATES: So if I am *dis*honest, then is that equally a reason for being dishonest: because I choose to be, because that is what I am, because that is now my being, since my being is constructed by my choices, whatever they are. Does that not logically follow?

SARTRE: Yes. You, Socrates, have chosen to be the slave of truth. You have chosen *not* to be dishonest. Others have chosen the opposite.

SOCRATES: But what do you say to them? Simply "different strokes for different folks", and that's all? Would you give a liar no reason at all to choose to be honest instead?

EHE, 45   SARTRE: Indeed I would—and I did. Didn't you read what I wrote? I said, **"the strictly coherent attitude is that of honesty."**

SOCRATES: But *why* choose "the strictly coherent attitude"? Suppose I don't *want* to be coherent? Why is coherence better than incoherence?

SARTRE: I cannot give you any objective, universally binding reason. The value of truth-telling is up to you. All values are. Your choice creates its own justification for yourself.

SOCRATES: Whatever your choice may be?

SARTRE: Yes. Whatever your choice may be. I deny that there is any pre-existing objective or external standard outside the choice that can judge it as right or wrong.

SOCRATES: We must explore that principle later: do choices create justifications and justice, or does justice judge choices? That is a very big question, both in importance and in extent. But we have not yet looked clearly at the narrower question of honesty and your justification for it in "coherence". Can you explain that, please? I do not see why you must choose honesty if you only want coherence. Can't some lies be quite coherent within themselves, consistent with themselves?

SARTRE: Yes, but not with the liar's mind and experience.

SOCRATES: Ah, so then there *is* some external standard outside the lie to judge it and condemn it, and to judge truth-telling as better. An objective standard. Even though it is only "the liar's own mind and experience".

SARTRE: I would not call that "an objective standard". It's not God, or "natural law", or some Platonic Idea of the Good, or the Ten Commandments, or anything like that. It's the individual's own mind and experience. I would not call that objective but subjective.

SOCRATES: Is the choice between honesty and dishonesty a choice between opposite values?

SARTRE: Of course.

SOCRATES: And is the choice between coherence and incoherence, between consistency and inconsistency, also a choice between opposite values?

SARTRE: Yes.

SOCRATES: And do you say that all values are subjective?

SARTRE: Yes. That is why I would not impose my personal values on you, or judge yours as objectively wrong, any more than I would judge your taste in cheese, or women.

SOCRATES: Oh, but you do. You do just that.

SARTRE: What! Where?

EHE, 45 SOCRATES: Why right here, in this book that you wrote, this book that we are exploring. You say: **"I maintain that there is dishonesty if I choose to state that certain values exist prior to me; it is self-contradictory for me to want them and at the same time state that they are imposed on me."** That seems pretty "judgmental" to me.

SARTRE: But that is not my attempt to impose my values on anyone else. The man who surrenders to *any* values as prior to him, whether the values are mine or God's, is dishonest. And dishonesty is inconsistency. For if these values are imposed on him, then they are not *his* will, but an other will. And if they *are* his will, then they are not imposed on him from another.

SOCRATES: I don't see how they can't be both.

SARTRE: How *can* they be? Haven't you read Kant? Your morality is either heteronomous or autonomous. Your values come either from your own will, freely, or from another's will, unfreely. How could they be both?

SOCRATES: They could be both if you *will* the will of the other.

SARTRE: Oh. But you can't do that and at the same time remain free. I will not compromise or limit or finitize my freedom.

SOCRATES: But you have already done just that, in saying that we *can't* do, that we aren't *free* to do, what most people believe we *are* free to do, namely to freely will the will of another, to freely choose to agree and believe and conform and obey the will of another, whether that other is man or God. You say we are *less* free than most people believe, not more; for you say we are not free to say "thy will be done."

But we will explore the question of freedom later. My question now is simply this: You would tell me that honesty is better than dishonesty simply because

it is coherent with my own subjective experience—
is that right?

SARTRE: Yes.

SOCRATES: And what if I say that it is *not* more coherent with my subjective experience?

SARTRE: Then for you that's what it is. That is your
truth. Truth is subjective. There is no impersonal,
objective, universal, unchangeable, absolute *a priori*
Truth for everyone.

SOCRATES: Not even the law of non-contradiction?

SARTRE: Not even that, if I choose to say No to it.
And I can. You see, Socrates, I am like Dostoyevski's
"Underground Man" in the Crystal Palace of Reason. I explode the crystal. You say to me that two and
two are four, and that is a fact. And I say to you that
I hate the fact that two and two are four, and *that*
is also a fact. You say to me that I contradict myself,
and I reply that that is precisely my glory. As the
American poet, Walt Whitman, wrote, "Do I contradict myself? Very well, then, I contradict myself.
I am large. I contain multitudes." You see, Socrates,
there stands before you an example of what you say is
impossible. I am a man who has chosen to contradict
himself if he wills to. It is possible, you see, to choose
to be self-contradictory. For if God does not exist,
all things are possible as well as permissible. There
is no *a priori* Truth for the same reason there is no *a
priori* Good: because **there is no infinite and perfect consciousness to think it.** "Objective Truth"
is just God without a face.

SOCRATES: I see. So atheism is your very first principle, and not deduced from any other, such as the problem of evil, or anything from science.

SARTRE: Yes. We have established that already.

SOCRATES: Let's see whether I have this right or not. I think I have discovered the chain of your logic. You reject objective values. And when asked why, you say because you think it is "dishonest" to accept them. And when asked why you reject dishonesty, you say that **"the strictly coherent attitude is that of honesty"**. And when asked why you reject incoherence, you say that there is no reason for coherency, because there is no God, no eternal Truth or eternal Being, and therefore no metaphysical basis for the law of non-contradiction.

EHE, 45

SARTRE: I affirm that chain of reasoning.

SOCRATES: So we have tracked the chain back to its first link, the absence of God.

SARTRE: We have. But that "tracking" is no great achievement. I said just that, explicitly, in many places. For instance, **"Existentialism is nothing else than an attempt to draw all the consequences of a coherent atheist position."** There's my one-sentence summary of existentialism. It took no clever piece of logical detective work on your part to discover what I had already given you. What's your point?

EHE, 51

SOCRATES: I just wanted to be totally clear and certain about that point before questioning it.

SARTRE: And what is your question about it now?

SOCRATES: It's just one little word in that wonderful one-sentence summary of Existentialism.

SARTRE: What word?

SOCRATES: "Consequences." It seems quite out of place. It assumes the principles of logic, and the law of non-contradiction, which you just rejected along with God.

SARTRE: Not at all. It fits perfectly. I embrace all the logical consequences of atheism, unlike the Enlightenment *philosophes*.

SOCRATES: But why? Why obey the law of non-contradiction? Why not be inconsistent?

SARTRE: We are arguing in a circle. You asked that before.

SOCRATES: And your answer then was that you could give no answer, no reason for being consistent.

SARTRE: Yes, and I still say that.

SOCRATES: But then you gave a *reason* for giving no reason, namely that God does not exist and therefore truth also does not exist—at least *a priori* truth, unchangeable truth, objective truth, universal truth. For there is no divine mind for these truths to be in.

SARTRE: That's right. I trace all my philosophy back to the absence of God, just as a theist traces all his philosophy back to God. So we are left with these two fundamental options, each quite consistent with itself and inconsistent with each other, like two different universes.

SOCRATES: And only one of these mental universes contains a God, or is the creation of a God, and therefore only one of them contains all the consequences of there being a God, such as objective truths and objective values.

SARTRE: That's right.

SOCRATES: And one of these consequences is the law of non-contradiction as a universal and objectively binding law over man's mind.

SARTRE: Correct again.

SOCRATES: Let me see whether I have your position clear in my own mind or not. Here you stand, an atheist. And here stands a theist before you. And each of us makes a choice, an opposite choice: God or no God. And each of us is responsible for that choice, and for all the consequences of that choice. Correct so far?

SARTRE: Yes.

SOCRATES: And one of the consequences of your atheistic choice is that there are no objective truths, and no objective values, and no human nature, and that existence is prior to essence.

SARTRE: We have gone over all that before. You are getting very tiresome, Socrates. What is your question?

SOCRATES: It is this: Why do you as an atheist treat one of the features you claim is valid only in the theistic universe as if it were equally valid in your atheistic universe? In fact, you treat it as if it were valid above or outside of both universes, as a standard for judging them and comparing them.

SARTRE: But I *don't* believe in any universal truth overarching all universes. That's my point. That's a consequence of atheism.

SOCRATES: I see. These other atheists, the rationalists of the Enlightenment, the *philosophes*, they did not realize this consequence, as you did, did they?

SARTRE: No, they didn't.

SOCRATES: Why didn't they?

SARTRE: They were not consistent. They did not follow out their atheism into all the logical consequences, as I did.

SOCRATES: So you are using the standard of logical consistency, the laws of logic, which you claim have absolute validity only within the theistic universe— you are using this "God without a face" to judge and condemn these *philosophes* as inconsistent and to justify yourself as consistent. And you are also using it as a standard to compare the atheistic universe and the theistic universe when you criticize the theist for being "inconsistent" when he claims that he freely chooses objective values and at the same time claims they are imposed on him by God.

SARTRE: Ah, I see what you are doing, Socrates: you are playing Cratylus to my Heraclitus.

SOCRATES: I *think* I know what you mean by that, but would you please spell it out for me?

SARTRE: Heraclitus taught that "everything flows", like a river; that there was no unchanging reality and therefore no unchanging truth except the law or "logos" of change itself. He said, "You can never step into the same river twice, for other and yet other waters are always flowing on." And his disciple Cratylus accused his teacher Heraclitus of inconsistency, both in theory and in practice. In theory, for Cratylus said that if Heraclitus is right, you couldn't even step into the same river *once*. And in practice, because if *everything* changes, then the meaning of speech and perhaps even the laws of thought change too (for speech is a kind of river). So Cratylus would not speak a word, but only move his little finger.

And now, it seems, you are trying to silence me by arguing that my very act of arguing, or speaking coherently and consistently, presupposes your God —with or without a face. So I am being inconsistent with my atheism even by speaking in a coherent way.

SOCRATES: That is exactly my question. Thank you for formulating it so clearly.

SARTRE: You're welcome.

SOCRATES: And your answer to it is—?

SARTRE: I am surprised you do not see it, Socrates. It's very obvious. You have accused me of inconsistency, and I answer: Guilty as charged! But in my court, what you call a crime is a heroic deed. My answer is Walt Whitman's answer. *Of course* I contradict myself. Whenever I want to! That is the privilege of an atheist, a privilege you sheepish theists have refused to accept. You freely sell your birthright of freedom and bow down to the tyranny of the laws of logic, laws which you have decreed yourself. You are the idolaters, not we atheists; you worship your own inventions, your own idols. We do not.

SOCRATES: How fascinating: the accusation of idolatry from an atheist! On earth, I was accused of atheism by idolaters. A double irony.

SARTRE: Is that the best you can do, Socrates? An *ad hominem?*

SOCRATES: That is not my answer.

SARTRE: Well? I'm waiting.

SOCRATES: Imagine a very primitive country that neither makes nor imports nor uses any kind of money. Now tell me: with no real money, how could any coin be counterfeit in that country?

SARTRE: It couldn't, of course.

SOCRATES: And counterfeit money is to real money as idols are to God?

SARTRE: The analogy seems apt.

SOCRATES: And an atheistic universe, without any God or gods at all, is like a country without any money at all. Is that a fair analogy?

SARTRE: I suppose so.

SOCRATES: Then tell me, how could I possibly commit idolatry in your atheistic universe? How can one sin against a God who does not exist?

SARTRE: One cannot, of course. But in *your* universe there *is* a God. So *you* can commit idolatry.

SOCRATES: But if there is a God, it is not idolatry to believe in objective truth and the laws of coherence and non-contradiction, for they stem from the divine nature.

SARTRE: So what?

SOCRATES: So whether there is or is not a God, in neither case can the believer in objective truth be committing idolatry.

SARTRE: Hmmm. . . .

SOCRATES: But we have again been diverted onto a long side road, though an important one. We should have been examining your book more closely.

4

"Being-in-itself" and
"Being-for-itself"

SOCRATES: I have been searching for your first principle, and I seem to have found *two* first principles, both in your book and in your conversation. You have admitted that atheism is your first principle, and that your system is nothing but the consequences of atheism. But you also say that the formula that **"existence precedes essence"** is **"the first principle of existentialism"**. The first "first principle" is about God, the second "first principle" is about man. Which is the real first principle?

EHE, 13, 15

SARTRE: Logically, atheism is first. As you have discovered, the rest of my philosophy follows logically from atheism. But I am not a logician first of all, and certainly not a theologian. I am an existentialist. And that is why I began with anthropology, not theology. I did not begin my book by asserting that God does not exist, but that existence precedes essence. That is a statement about man, not God; about the self, or subject, or **"being-for-itself"**. And that is important, that makes a great difference, because it defends my atheism from the charge of arbitrariness. It grounds it in human experience.

SOCRATES: That is what I thought you would say. That is why I did not pursue the purely logical question further.

SARTRE: You pursued it far enough, I think, to exhaust most people's patience! But I commend you for understanding that my philosophy is based first of all on experience; that I am a phenomenologist, not a logician. Frankly, Socrates, I had thought *you* were merely a logician, and I was rather surprised that after you got me to admit that atheism was my first principle, my first premise, you didn't challenge me to *prove* that premise.

SOCRATES: How would you have answered that challenge?

SARTRE: I would have refused to do so.

SOCRATES: And what would you have said if I then accused you of being as arbitrary as the man who begins with the first principle that snakes are gods, or that God is a snake, but who refused to prove that principle? What would you have said if I had accused you of giving atheism as your reason for everything else but giving no reason for your atheism? Would you have given a reason or not?

You seem to be in a dilemma here. For if you answer yes, then I ask you what the reason can be. From what prior premise could you possibly derive your *first* premise? And if your existentialism is ultimately based on this *reason*, then how is it existentialism rather than rationalism?

But if you answer no, if you say that your atheism is *not* based on any reason, then your argument loses its power to convince anyone else and becomes merely an expression of your own private feeling or willing. Then it seems to be based either on your feeling of nausea at existence, your feeling-experience of the absurdity of existence; or else on your will's resentment at God for not letting you be totally free, something like Nietzsche's "will to power", with its stunning satire of all arguments: "I will now *disprove* the existence of all gods. If there were gods, how could I bear not to be a god? *Consequently* there are no gods." Which horn of the dilemma do you choose?

SARTRE: I would not repudiate that answer of Nietzsche's. It is a striking passage, isn't it?

SOCRATES: As "striking" as a blow to the brain.

SARTRE: I would call it a noble act of will. But it is only an act of will. I add to it an intellectual reason. And I also stand by my feeling of the absurdity of existence as a basis for my atheism. For that feeling is to me as self-justifying as a physical sensation, and it can be that for anyone who has the eye to see. But this too is not a *reason*. It is an intuition. So I add a reason to these two things, these other two bases for my atheism, the willing and the feeling. And my reason is in my analysis of **"being-in-itself"** and **"being-for-itself"**.

SOCRATES: If you give a reason for your atheism, why doesn't that make you a rationalist rather than an existentialist?

SARTRE: Because it is not a *proof*, not a logical proof, but a reason that is grounded in experience, in a phenomenological analysis of experience.

SOCRATES: Could you explain what you mean by "phenomenology"?

SARTRE: I'd be glad to. It's a rather long and murky story. Let me start . . .

SOCRATES: No, don't start, stop! Could you explain it very briefly and clearly?

SARTRE: I don't think so. Which would you prefer, brief or clear?

SOCRATES: Brief, please.

SARTRE: Phenomenology is a logic of phenomena rather than a logic of propositions.

SOCRATES: Well, that's brief anyway. Perhaps it will become clear as we do it. These two fundamental categories of yours—they sound quite Cartesian. Do you mean the same thing by **"being-in-itself"** and **"being-for-itself"** as Descartes meant by "extended substance" and "thinking substance", or matter and mind?

SARTRE: No. His dualism was in the realm of objective metaphysics. Mine is a dualism between the whole objective realm and the subjective.

SOCRATES: So **"being-for-itself"** means the subjective, or subjectivity?

SARTRE: It means the reality of a subject of consciousness, not just the *attitude* of being "subjective" as opposed to the attitude of being "objective". *All* attitudes are subjective; that is, they are attitudes of a subject. Mountains have no attitudes, only altitudes.

SOCRATES: So **"being-in-itself"** is the realm of consciousness? That sounds Cartesian.

SARTRE: It is the realm of *self*-consciousness. And also
freedom. Animals do not fall under it. They have a
kind of consciousness but not self-consciousness, and
not freedom.

SOCRATES: I see. That seems fairly clear. Why did
you invent those two terms, with their contrasting
prepositions?

SARTRE: Let's begin with being-in-itself. I say "in"
to show that being-in-itself rests in its own essence.
It is compete, finished, full of itself. It is perfect. It
has no identity crisis. It is totally sincere. It is simply
what it is. It has no self, and no self-consciousness, no
freedom and no future, no hopes or dreams or values,
no inner life, no power to be anything else. It is determined. It is not in relationships with other beings.
It is never "here", just "there". This all applies both
to physical objects, like stones, and mental objects,
like triangles. Both are examples of being-in-itself.

Being-for-itself, on the other hand, first exists,
without any essence. It is always "on the way", *en
passant*, incomplete, imperfect, unfinished, *not*-itself.
It is always in an identity crisis because it *makes* its
own identity, its own essence. Its identity is not determined beforehand.

SOCRATES: So once you have these two categories,
what do you do with them? What propositions do
you construct with these terms?

SARTRE: These two propositions first of all. The first
one formulates the difference between them. It is that

Being-in-itself is what it is, while being-for-itself is not what it is. The second applies them to us, and says that *For being-for-itself, essence is prior to existence.*

SOCRATES: I see. So being-for-itself is your term for human consciousness and freedom, while being-in-itself is your term for the objects of human consciousness and freedom—is that right?

SARTRE: Yes.

SOCRATES: Why do you use such abstract terms?

SARTRE: To make the point that man's very mode of being is different from everything else in the universe. Take that paper-cutter, for instance. Or take a natural object, like a rock, or even a dog. To say that it is simply a being-in-itself is to say that throughout its career in time, throughout its concrete, factual "life", or "existence", *it is always what it is*, its existence is wholly determined by its essence. An acorn must be an acorn, and must become an oak. No oak can be non-oak, no dog can be un-doggy. But humans can be inhuman. For our very *being* is different from the being of everything else in the universe. Being-for-itself is always *on the way* to becoming itself, but it is never quite wholly there, never totally itself. Thus I say it is "not" what it is—that is, in its concrete, actual existence it is never identical with, and never simply determined by, and never wholly explainable by, its essence, its given, prior concept, its design or ideal, like the idea of the paper-cutter in the mind of its designer. Unlike artificial or natural objects, we are not *made*. We *make ourselves* what we are. Thus **"being-for-itself"** is another name for freedom.

SOCRATES: The point seems quite simple but very abstract. How about a concrete example to illustrate?

SARTRE: Nothing is easier. Take my famous description of the waiter in the café:

BN, 59
Look at this waiter who is serving us. His gestures are lively, insistent, and a little too precise. He comes to get his orders a little too quickly, he bends down a little too readily; his voice, his glance are a little too solicitous. Now he is coming back with the drinks, imitating in his walk the inflexible rigor of an automaton, carrying his tray with the agility of a conjurer. . . . His whole manner is a performance. . . . He is play-acting . . . what then is his role? Whom is he impersonating? The answer is simple: he is impersonating a waiter in a café.

You see, he is trying to attain the being-in-itself of a *waiter*. But he is in fact always being-for-itself. Yet every attempt, of ours as well as his, outside the café as well as in it, is aimed at some being-in-itself, at some ideal, some idea, some concept. That paradox is the point of my formula for being-for-itself: *it is not what it is*. It is not, in its existence, what it is in its essence. It is not, as being-for-itself, the being-in-itself that it always seeks to be and identifies with. Its real identity is to have no such positive identity, no essence.

SOCRATES: Thank you for that explanation. Do you understand why I asked for it, why I steered our conversation away from the easier, less technical ter-

minology of *Existentialism and Human Emotions*, the
book we were investigating, and into the notoriously
difficult *Being and Nothingness*, so that we could understand your two fundamental categories of being-
in-itself and being-for-itself?

SARTRE: You tell me, Socrates. It was your steering.

SOCRATES: It was because we traced your whole philosophy back to your first principle, atheism, and then
we asked whether this first principle was purely willful and arbitrary or whether there was some reason
for it, or at least some intelligible explanation for it.
And you said yes, there was, and that it was precisely
this: your analysis of being-for-itself and being-in-
itself. Is that a fair summary of the logic of our investigation so far?

SARTRE: Yes.

SOCRATES: And now, to anyone who might not be
able to understand and follow your abstract descrip-
tions of being-in-itself and being-for-itself, could we
say to them, speaking in a more simple and concrete
way, that *being-for-itself is conscious and free but always
imperfect*, always trying to make itself something else,
while *being-in-itself is perfect*, perfectly itself, finished,
but not conscious and free. Could we say that?

SARTRE: Yes, we could say that as a fair approxima-
tion.

SOCRATES: And these are the only two possible modes
of being, correct? Or is there a third?

SARTRE: These are the only two. There can be no
third.

SOCRATES: So there is no "being itself" over and above these two modes of being? Nothing for both of the two to participate in and share and be united in?

SARTRE: No. No God, no Hegelian Absolute, no Platonic Idea.

SOCRATES: Not even an Aristotelian universal form?

SARTRE: Not even that. That would be too much like God.

SOCRATES: But *why* not? Why no being-itself, but only being-in-itself or being-for-itself? You see why I am asking this question "why?"—because I want to find out whether your first starting point is simply willful and arbitrary—like Nietzsche's "how could I bear not to be a god?"—or whether you have some reason for it.

SARTRE: It is both. It is a choice, an existential act of will, not a proof. Yet I also have reason for it. And my reason is found in my phenomenological analysis of human experience. And that analysis is summarized in being-for-itself versus being-in-itself.

SOCRATES: That is what I thought. And could you summarize that reason now, or that analysis, or whatever is your justification for rejecting God or anything like God, any being-itself over and above being-for-itself and being-in-itself?

SARTRE: Nothing could be easier. There is only being-for-itself and being-in-itself because a being must be either conscious and free or not, and it must be either perfectly finished or not. That is simply the logical

"Law of Excluded Middle": *Either p or not p.* It is not possible to conceive or imagine a third possibility.

SOCRATES: Then how did Heidegger do it?

SARTRE: What do you mean?

SOCRATES: What you mean by **"being-for-itself"**, or subjectivity, corresponds pretty closely to what Heidegger meant by *Dasein*, or human existence; and what you mean by **"being-in-itself"** corresponds pretty closely to what he meant by *Seiendes*, objects, things-that-are. Wouldn't you say that?

SARTRE: No, I would not say that.

SOCRATES: But surely there is a parallel, a similarity?

SARTRE: Structurally, yes. Functionally, no. What he does with his categories is very different than what I do with mine.

SOCRATES: But the categories themselves are fairly parallel. If they were boxes, the two of you would agree on what belongs in each box, even though the labels on the boxes are different.

SARTRE: I will grant that much, yes.

SOCRATES: But Heidegger also had a third category: *Sein*, being-itself. And this was what he said his whole philosophy was about. This is what he was always trying to let unfold, or manifest, in one way or another.

SARTRE: And he was wrong! There is no such thing as being.

SOCRATES: That sounds like the formula for metaphysical nihilism: "there is no such thing as being."

You are a Nihilist, then? Where others see Being, you see Nothing?

SARTRE: The word "nihilism" has pejorative connotations. I am not a bomb-throwing hater and destroyer of all things human. In fact, I am a true humanist. As I wrote, my philosophy **"is the only one that grants man truly human dignity, that does not reduce him to an object"**.

EHE, 37

SOCRATES: Whether that is so or not, you are a Nihilist in the technical and metaphysical sense I just defined, are you not? You say there is no Being, no Being-itself, only being-for-itself and being-in-itself, and these two can never participate in a common third.

SARTRE: That is correct. I am a dualist, not a monist. There is no One above these Two.

SOCRATES: Now let us remember *why* we steered our investigation into these difficult waters. We had to explore this ultimate dualism of yours to see whether it provided a reason for your atheism.

SARTRE: Yes.

SOCRATES: And now we seem to have found the reason. It is quite clear: being-for-itself is conscious and free but not perfect, while being-in-itself is perfect but not conscious and free. But "God" means a being that is both totally perfect and totally conscious and free.

SARTRE: Exactly, Socrates! So the very concept of God is self-contradictory. It is the confusion of the two ultimate categories. It is a metaphysical oxymoron.

SOCRATES: So you have there a kind of ontological argument for the nonexistence of God, the same kind of argument as St. Anselm's famous "ontological argument" *for* the existence of God. He said atheism is self-contradictory, and you say theism is.

SARTRE: Yes. And my argument is better than his because he was limiting himself to objects, while I added another category to his, the category of subjects, or being-for-itself. He said God must exist because God has all perfections and objective existence is a perfection. But he forgot subjective existence. He worked only within the realm of concepts, or being-in-itself. So my categories include his, but his do not include mine. My argument relativizes his, as Einstein relativized Newton.

SOCRATES: I understand.

SARTRE: I am very pleased that you understand that, Socrates. But I am not surprised. For you were caught in a similar dualism in your own culture when it came to the gods, if what Plato wrote about you was true. . . .

SOCRATES: Some of it was, anyway. Which part are you thinking of?

SARTRE: You transformed religion because you replaced imperfect gods with perfect Ideas. You replaced illogically-imagined divine being-for-itself with logically-conceived divine being-in-itself. You replaced imperfect persons like Zeus and Apollo and

Aphrodite with perfect impersonal essences like Justice and Truth and Beauty. You did that, didn't you?

SOCRATES: Plato did, anyway. It doesn't matter who first said it, only whether it's true.

SARTRE: And the truth is that *both* Zeus and Justice, both Apollo and Truth, both gods and perfect Platonic Ideas, were projections from your human experience, and not realities. But the projections are perfectly explained by my categories. For we experience being-for-itself in ourselves as persons, so we imagine and invent more perfect versions of these, divine persons in the heavens, and we call them gods, and worship the works of our own minds. It's only one step up from pagans worshipping idols of wood or stone, the works of their own hands. And we also experience the other mode of being, being-in-itself, as the mental or physical objects of our own thinking and sensing. This includes the ideas our minds create. So you imagined (or Plato imagined) more perfect versions of these ideas and claimed that they existed independently of the mind, in eternity, as unchanging divine ideas, not changing human ideas. They were ideas with a capital "I".

Both gods and Platonic Ideas are superstitions, projections, idols. But the most impossible idea ever conceived is neither of these two; it is the absolutely self-contradictory idea of God as the perfect person, the eternal consciousness, the being-for-itself that is also being-in-itself, the being in which subject equals object, existence equals essence, "I" equals "Being": the Being whose name is "I AM".

SOCRATES: Where do you think that idea came from, if it is so absurd? It is a very popular one, this idea of a perfect God.

SARTRE: I can explain that too. It comes from our deepest desire, which in turn comes from the very structure of our existence. Others say the God-idea came from external social conditions, or priestly power plays, or some genetic defect in brain wiring. I give the idea far more weight than that. It comes from the fundamental project of human reality, from the very structure of human existence. Man is the being that wants to be God. He wants to be perfect without losing his personhood. And that is impossible. So in our very being is the desire for the impossible. That is why I say that **"man is a useless passion."**   EHE, 90

SOCRATES: You sound almost like Saint Augustine!

SARTRE: What? Why in the world would you say that? He gave himself up totally to that repressive and dehumanizing superstition. I liberate mankind from it. Why would you confuse an atheist with a saint?

SOCRATES: Because you said that in our very being is the desire for the impossible. Augustine said almost exactly the same thing: "Our hearts are restless until they rest in Thee." But it is impossible for us to get ourselves to God, to lift ourselves up by our own bootstraps. That's why Augustine said our only hope was divine grace. He would quite agree with you that the desire for God is built into the very structure of human existence; and he would also say that we are a kind of living self-contradiction: we *must* be perfect

but we *can't* be perfect. He would quite agree with
your definition of man as "a useless passion", for two
reasons.

First, that we *are* our passion, that our very being
is our deepest love, and that our hearts are restless
until they rest in God—whether they ever do rest in
God or not, and even whether God exists or not.

And second, that without divine grace, divine mir-
acle, our passion for God is useless, hopeless—but
not for the very abstract and logical reason that
you gave—because the idea of God is logically self-
contradictory—but for a more existential reason,
which he called "Original Sin".

So whether you are right or wrong about God, I
think Augustine is more of an existentialist than you
are. And I think you are a far more religious philosopher than most so-called religious philosophers.

SARTRE: No, no, Socrates. A moment ago I thought
you understood me very well—and you did seem to
understand what I mean by my two categories. But
now I see that you do not understand me at all when
it comes to this desire for God. Here is your mistake,
Socrates. You confuse two things. The desire that I
say is built into man's being is not *that God should be*
but *that I should be God*. It is not religion but irreligion
—blasphemy is what religious people would call it—
that is the essential human project.

SOCRATES: I see. But what these two things have in
common—the desire that God should be, and the
desire that I should be God—is the assumption that
God is possible. And you deny that assumption, do
you not?

SARTRE: I do.

SOCRATES: And why? Because the idea of God—the God of the Bible, anyway, as distinct from the gods of pagan religion or the Ideas of pagan philosophy— does not fit into either of your two categories, and there can be no third because it is self-contradictory.

SARTRE: Yes. That is what you called my Anselmian "ontological argument for the nonexistence of God".

SOCRATES: But if that is the basis for your atheism, if that is your first principle and starting point, then both you and Anselm are judging human experience by a set of abstract categories, while both Nietzsche and Augustine are doing the opposite. So they are the existentialists, while you are the rationalist.

SARTRE: Is this supposed to be an insult? Or a refutation? Why should I care whether you call my philosophy rationalism or not? That's label, not substance.

SOCRATES: No, it is substance. The question is not: Do you fit the label of "rationalist" or not? I will grant you freedom from the label if you wish. That is merely a question of shuffling categories. But so is your argument against God. Both you and Anselm argue–against God or for God–simply by arranging your categories so as to logically exclude theism or to logically exclude atheism.

SARTRE: What is wrong with my categories?

SOCRATES: My point is not that your *categories* are wrong, but your reason for inventing them. You see, I'm trying to find the very first starting point of your existentialism. And the parallel with Anselm gives me the answer, I think. Just as Anselm invented his proof *not* in order to find out whether God existed or not, as if he was really wondering, really doubting, but to explain and justify his prior conviction that He did, so you invented your two categories, and defined them as you did, just to keep God out, to explain *your* prior conviction of atheism. So atheism is your *a priori* after all. It is not justified by any prior reason. It is as arbitrary as Nietzsche's, only less passionate.

SARTRE: You have been most un-Socratic all this time, Socrates. Now this is the last straw. The man whom the oracle declared wise because he knew that he had no wisdom now claims to understand not only my public argument but also my deepest reasons, my private motives, my heart!

SOCRATES: I do not claim that. I analyze only your words. And I see there no neutral, secular starting point from which you derive your atheism, but only your religious starting point of atheism itself. You said there *was* such a neutral starting point, namely the analysis of human experience from which you derived your categories, and then your atheism. But the categories seem designed *for* atheism, and *from* a prior theism. They are not the basis of your atheism, as you said, but vice versa. So how could a theist argue with you? You and he would just be two preachers, not two philosophers.

SARTRE: You are wrong: this is philosophy, not preaching. But you are right that my atheism is my starting point, and the reason for everything else. Everything else, even my fundamental categories, *can* be derived from atheism. But my categories are also my starting point, and atheism can also be derived from them.

SOCRATES: Isn't that arguing in a circle? Atheism is the reason for the categories and the categories are the reason for atheism.

SARTRE: It is a single starting point but expressed in two different ways. My categories are the abstract version, and my atheism is the concrete version.

SOCRATES: But that still leaves your starting point unjustified, and unargued. Anyone could start with another set of categories if he wanted to. In fact, most philosophers have done just that, for thousands of years.

SARTRE: They have done that, of course, and I am the culmination of that historical process, as you were the beginning. Philosophy begins with Socrates and ends with Sartre! I am your final offspring, Socrates.

SOCRATES: Oh, God, forgive me! What have I done? You told me, "Know thyself", and I now find the answer: I am Doctor Frankenstein!

5

Method

SARTRE: I do not accept your characterization of my fundamental categories as arbitrary, Socrates. They are based on experience. They do not come from an *a priori* metaphysics but *a posteriori* from a phenomenological anthropology, an analysis of the phenomena of ordinary human experience.

SOCRATES: Then why do you always turn to *extra*ordinary human experiences, in fact extraordinarily *pathological* experiences, as your data base? Your protagonist Roquentin in *Nausea* finds everything totally absurd and meaningless, even suicide—surely this is not typical. The three people who torture each other in your earthly hell in *No Exit* are not typical people but extraordinarily pitiful and perverse. Why didn't you choose three ordinary people if you wanted to make a point you claim is universal?

SARTRE: I think they *are* ordinary. We are all "pitiful and perverse". But my fundamental categories do not depend on these three people. They are universal.

SOCRATES: But the experience from which you most famously and clearly derive these categories is hardly a universal experience. It is the experience of being seen by another as you are looking through a keyhole surreptitiously, eavesdropping.

SARTRE: Sometimes, unusual or extraordinary experiences reveal more clearly what is universal but hidden, as the element radium reveals more clearly the radioactivity that is hidden in all elements, or as Hitler reveals the "Hitler in ourselves", to quote Max Picard's title. Even theists like Dostoyevski and Kierkegaard see that point.

SOCRATES: That is true. Do you still claim that your real basis and starting point is existentialism, not rationalism; anthropology, not theology; phenomenology, not metaphysics; experience, not logic?

SARTRE: I do.

SOCRATES: Well, then, I suppose we had better restart our investigation there.

SARTRE: It's about time! I do not call it "anthropology", though, but "existential psychology". "Anthropology" assumes that *anthropos* has a *logos*, that man has a nature.

SOCRATES: So you claim that all men are individuals with no human nature in common.

SARTRE: Yes. All men are different.

SOCRATES: Then how can we call them all "men"?

SARTRE: Speech is sloppy. It is practical to be sloppy. All language falsifies, except proper names. Remember that scene in Hemingway where he is bemoaning the absurdity of war and says that the only words he can find any meaning in any more are the names of the dead?

SOCRATES: That is a powerful scene.

SARTRE: How do you know that scene? Has everyone up here read everything ever written down there? Or should I say "down here" and "up there"?

SOCRATES: We know all that we need to know. And whether it is "up" or "down" will be your choice.

SARTRE: I'll take "Down", please. I hate heights.

SOCRATES: You will not be allowed to be so hasty as that. That is why I am here.

SARTRE: I knew it. It is just as I wrote in *No Exit*. Soon, a third will show up, and I will torture him as you are torturing me.

SOCRATES: You will not believe this, but there is One who cannot be tortured. You cannot make Him a being-in-itself. He is a mirror who reflects everything back. And I am supposed to be doing a little of His work right now. So let us return to that work. I will not be diverted from what is necessary.

SARTRE: I see. I suppose I have no choice in the matter.

SOCRATES: You do not.

SARTRE: I do not *see*?

SOCRATES: No, you *do* see. You do not have any *choice* in that matter. In the matter of seeing, I mean. This is the place where you *must* see, eventually.

SARTRE: Then this *is* Hell, as I thought. Well, let's get on with it. I was saying that "man" is sloppy speech, as proper names are not.

SOCRATES: But even sloppy speech can be meaningful. How do you account for the fact that we all do use universal words and concepts like "man" and "human nature" meaningfully?

SARTRE: It's shorthand. Abbreviations. Short-cuts.

SOCRATES: This is the old dispute about universals. You are a Nominalist: you believe that universals are only *nomina*, names.

SARTRE: Yes. Do you want to go back to the Middle Ages and review that old scholastic dispute? Or do you want to explore my book?

SOCRATES: That is like asking whether I want to talk about ancient Roma or modern Rome. It is all part of one history, and the old issues always lie at the base of the new ones as the ruins of an old city always lie under the buildings of the new city. But we need not go into the history of philosophy now. There will be plenty of time later for intellectual archaeology. We will just explore your present philosophy today.

SARTRE: That's what I thought your task was: to explore my book, not others' books.

SOCRATES: It is.

SARTRE: Then let us explore it in its own terms. I began not with metaphysical categories but with immediate experience, as Descartes did. I wrote,

There can be no other truth to take off from than this: *I think, therefore I exist.* There we have the absolute truth of consciousness becoming aware of itself. . . . Outside the Cartesian *cogito* all views are only probable, and . . . to describe the probable, you must first have a firm hold on the true.

EHE, 36

SOCRATES: You contrast "the true" here not to "the false" but to "the probable". Why?

SARTRE: Because like Descartes, I demand not just truth but certainty.

SOCRATES: Why?

SARTRE: Because what most men call wisdom or tradition or experience is for the most part a deliberate lie to one's self, a way of denying or avoiding or concealing the absurdity and meaninglessness of human life.

SOCRATES: I see. Is that why you cultivate a "hermeneutic of suspicion" and treat all ideas as false until proved true, as Descartes did, rather than treating ideas as true until proved false, as I did?

SARTRE: Yes, but for Descartes this was a mere method, something artificial, a way of applying the scientific method to philosophy. For me, it extends beyond that. It is not just a method but the nature of philosophical thought itself. And it is not just philosophy but life.

SOCRATES: Why? Why is this not simply the imposition of your personal temperament? Do you claim it is rationally justified?

SARTRE: I do.

SOCRATES: I think you can guess what my next question is going to be.

SARTRE: The justification is this: I am painfully aware of the mechanisms of self-deception. That is why, for instance, it makes absolutely no difference whether the Christians are right when they say there has been a divine revelation to correct fallen human reason and give us wisdom from above. For, as I wrote in my book,

> **The existentialist does not think that man is going to help himself by finding in the world some omen by which to orient himself. Because he thinks that man will interpret the omen to suit himself.**   EHE, 23

SOCRATES: I still do not see how you escape the charge that your whole philosophy is nothing but the projection of your peculiar personality, and thus not one whit more valid than a philosophy that was the projection of an opposite personality type. A saint would begin with trust, and that is not proof, that is not justified; but you begin with mistrust, and that is also not proof, and not justified. A saint's philosophy would be ordered toward hope, yours is ordered toward despair. A saint would center on love as the fundamental human relationship; you center on the torture of dehumanization and depersonalization and objectification. Thus to the saint, Heaven is not only God but also other people; to you, **"Hell is other people."** Why is your philosophy any more true or valid or compelling than its opposite? You see, I am only applying your own "hermeneutic of suspicion".

SARTRE: And it is perfectly valid for you do to so! And perfectly valid for the saint to create his own transvaluation of my values, or for me to transvalue his. Do you see what we are doing now? Exactly what I claim we are doing always: we are each creating his own values and his own criteria of validity. I do not impose my values universally.

SOCRATES: But suppose I say that I am *not* doing that? Suppose I say I speak not for myself but for Truth? You cannot answer me by simply retreating into "different strokes for different folks, so we can't argue". For if you do, then you are imposing that individualism of yours *universally*. But you just said "I do *not* impose my values universally."

SARTRE: Values have to be created by individuals. But they do not have to impose those values on others.

SOCRATES: But you are now using your value system, which claims that values are created by individuals, to settle the dispute between yourself and me, between your belief that values are relative to individuals and my belief that they are not. So you are making one of the two boxers into the referee.

SARTRE: I am indeed! But so are you, in exactly the opposite way, by assuming the necessity of an objective referee, and even the possibility of an objective referee, which I deny.

SOCRATES: But if there is no objective referee, how can the fight be judged? We are arguing, after all, and that cannot happen unless we are appealing to some common standard and each of us is claiming that he meets that standard better than the other. That is the phenomenology of all argument.

SARTRE: All right, but the standard is not some objective and universal truth, but *mastery*. Each of us wants the mastery, each wants to win, each wants to be God. But the other stands in the way.

SOCRATES: Speak for yourself, Jean-Paul. I do not want mastery, I only want truth. And I certainly don't want to be God.

SARTRE: You only illustrate my point: we deceive ourselves about what we really want.

SOCRATES: But if we deceive ourselves, we fail to know the truth about ourselves. And if we fail to know the truth about ourselves, there must be some truth about ourselves that we fail to know. And if there is some truth about ourselves that we fail to know, there must be objective truth. For "subjective truth" is only the truth we know, or will.

SARTRE: Clever syllogisms, Socrates. But you cannot deny that your very argument for "objective truth" is motivated by your will that your conclusion be true, and that it thus conquer mine. For you *do* want to be God. Your very choice to posit "objective truth" comes from your subjectivity. You know where you want to go, and then you find the best way to get there. You judge your reasons by your conclusion, even when you claim to be judging your conclusion by your reasons. Your so-called objective and impersonal logic is a fake, a mask, a self-deception.

SOCRATES: Alas, I fear we will never get anywhere if we keep arguing like this about the relation between persons and arguments, or subjectivity and objectivity. It's like the puzzle in nineteenth-century philosophy that they called "the ontological-epistemological circle": *being* has to judge *knowing* and yet *knowing* has to judge *being*. Being surrounds knowing because all knowing is a knowing of some being; but knowing also surrounds being because whenever you point to any being, you are *knowing* it.

Or it is like the older puzzle in ancient philosophy about the reason and the senses: you can't get any premises to reason from except from the senses, but you can't learn anything from the senses unless your sense experience is structured and interpreted by reason.

SARTRE: How do *you* solve those dilemmas, Socrates?

SOCRATES: I will not tell you that now. No more diversions. Let us just bypass that question for now, and instead of arguing about *how* to do philosophy, whether it should be objectively or subjectively, let's just *do* some. I am impatient to explore your answer to my favorite question, "Know thyself."

SARTRE: Explore away, Socrates, but you will never escape any of those circular puzzles.

SOCRATES: Perhaps not. And perhaps you will never escape me.

SARTRE: If so, I was right in the first place: this is Hell.

6

Man (and Woman)

SOCRATES: Your basic view of human nature is—that it does not exist. Is that right?

SARTRE: *Man* exists. That is enough.

SOCRATES: But what do you and I have in common if not human nature?

SARTRE: The human condition. Not some substance, or essence, or form. That would be Platonic idealism. I reject that absolutely.

SOCRATES: But *why* do you say man has no substance or essence or form?

SARTRE: Because that would give him a fixed identity like a stone; it would make him an object, one object among others in nature. If man has a nature, then man does not transcend nature. But man transcends nature. Therefore man has no nature. How's that for a syllogism?

SOCRATES: It's a syllogism, all right, but I am surprised at your second premise, that "man transcends nature."

SARTRE: Why?

SOCRATES: Because it sounds like the philosophy you said you reject absolutely a moment ago: Platonic idealism.

SARTRE: You misunderstand me, Socrates. When I say that "man transcends nature", I do not mean what Plato or the Christians mean: that he has an immortal soul, that he is something like a god, or made in God's image. Man transcends nature by his freedom from being a nature, an entity, an object, a being-in-itself. He is free, he is empty.

SOCRATES: So Man transcends Nature not by what he is—his nature—but by what he is not.

SARTRE: Yes.

SOCRATES: So his transcendence, his "moreness", consists in his "lessness".

SARTRE: That is a paradox, but it is true. We are free because we are empty.

SOCRATES: You seem to have much in common with Buddha. He too taught that the self was insubstantial, empty. He said we could reach this consciousness of emptiness by detachment from all desires.

SARTRE: Ah, yes, Buddhism: the philosophy of the ticket stub.

SOCRATES: What do you mean by that?

SARTRE: Haven't you ever read the message on a ticket stub? It says "void if detached". But seriously, I think your supposed resemblance between myself and Buddha is more apparent than real. For one thing, Buddha attacked the desires; I do not. I say man constitutes himself by his desires and wills and projects. For another thing, Buddha declared individuality to be an illusion. I say it is man's ultimate reality. Finally, Buddha seems to have been a monist, a pantheist: he believed that all is really one, and there is no many. I am the opposite: a nominalist, a pluralist: we are many, there is no one, no single reality that we share, not even a common "human nature".

SOCRATES: But you do see the self as a kind of bubble, as Buddha does, empty of substance.

SARTRE: Yes, but it is full of energy. The passion to blow up the bubble, to expand it—this is what I call the will to action. I exalt that, while Buddha denounced it, for he denounced all desires.

SOCRATES: "The will to action" sounds very much like Nietzsche's "will to power". Do you know what happens to every bubble when it expands enough?

SARTRE: Yes. It pops. It dies. As we do.

SOCRATES: But only if it is foolish enough to keep blowing itself up.

SARTRE: You can't argue from an analogy, Socrates. You should know that, of all people.

SOCRATES: It was not an argument, it was a warning.

SARTRE: Now you sound more like a preacher than a philosopher.

SOCRATES: Before I am a philosopher, I am a human being. And so are you.

SARTRE: Yes, I am. And every human being is a bubble. And you can't get inside my bubble, and I can't get inside yours. There's nothing inside anyway.

SOCRATES: If that is so, then all we can do with our "will to action", the only meaning we can give to our lives, is for each of us to expand the inner emptiness and meaninglessness of his bubble out into the equally empty and meaningless outer emptiness.

SARTRE: A striking analogy, Socrates. And I will give you another, which is an analogy to that analogy: this endless expansion into emptiness is exactly what the entire universe has been doing for about fifteen billion years, according to our modern astronomers.

SOCRATES: Then where do you see any meaning in our empty lives?

SARTRE: Objectively, there is none. None is *given* to us because there is no God, no divine Ideas, no divine Law, and no human nature. Besides, even if there *were* any of those things, it would be incompatible with our freedom for us to *receive* them, passively, as the paper receives the ink. That is why I say life is "absurd". But this is not demeaning, but ennobling and freeing. It is the only view of man that does not reduce him to an object.

SOCRATES: But it does something worse than that. It reduces him to meaninglessness and hopelessness in his life, in his practice. I thought you existentialists were more concerned with practice than with theory.

SARTRE: We are. And it is in the practical realm that meaning emerges. My view is ennobling because it emerges from us, not from nature. Even though objectively there is no meaning, subjectively there *is* meaning because we create it.

SOCRATES: Even though both we and the universe are empty bubbles?

SARTRE: Yes. We launch meanings, like rockets, out into the emptiness, from our own emptiness.

SOCRATES: How can an empty man make an empty universe to be full of meaning? How can nothing make something, or more make less? That seems to violate the principle of causality.

SARTRE: Because man *is* his choices, his projects, his launchings. Man is the sum of his actions. In creating his worlds, he *creates* his meanings.

SOCRATES: Like God.

SARTRE: Yes, like God. Aquinas defined God as pure act, with no potentiality. That is how I define man. As I wrote, **"Man is nothing else but what he makes of himself."** And again, **"Man is nothing more than . . . the ensemble of his acts, nothing else than his life."** My being is my life. I *am* my life.

EHE, 15
EHE, 32

SOCRATES: When most people say "my life" they mean both what they do and what they suffer, the active and the passive, what they make happen and what happens to them. But I think you mean by "my life" only my free, conscious choices and acts and projects, and not any of the things that are imposed upon me without my free choice or consciousness, like my genes, or my siblings, or my date of birth— is that correct?

SARTRE: That is correct.

SOCRATES: Why do you say that?

SARTRE: You philosophers who believe in immortality, you Platonists and Christians, should agree with that. You say "you can't take it with you" when you die. Let's analyze that saying for a moment. What is the "you" and what is the "it"? Surely the "it" is everything that is being-in-itself, an object, a part of nature or caused by nature, like the things you mentioned: your genes, your siblings, and your date of birth. You did not choose them, and therefore they are not a part of your being, your existence—your "soul", as you would call it. The "it" that "you can't take with you" is not yourself; but the "you" who can't take "it" with you *is* your self. You must understand that, Socrates. For you believe in life after death, you believe that you *can*, and indeed *must*, take your "you" with you to the Last Judgment. And that "you" is your free choices. That is what you will be judged on, according to your belief system.

For instance, take a man who is born blind, and who chooses to use his blindness to help other blind men because he believes in the Golden Rule. Let us say that his personality and example inspires one other blind man, who has a scientific mind, to invent some new device to help many other blind men. When the first man dies, you would say that he takes with him to the Last Judgment his self, his character, the kind of person he has made himself into by his acts; and that is what is judged. But he cannot take with him the second blind man, the scientist, or the device that the scientist has invented, or the many other blind men who are helped by it. All those things remain in the world of the living. To the first man, who is judged, they are all part of the "it" that he can't take with him.

Now it seems to me that that is exactly what Platonists and Christians are saying. So I don't know why they see my philosophy as so terribly threatening to them. Of course I do not believe in God or life after death or a last judgment; but as far as who we are in this life is concerned, I think we have the same idea.

SOCRATES: Do *they* think your idea is much the same as theirs?

SARTRE: No. They think we have a great difference of opinion.

SOCRATES: Then we should explore this difference of opinion about whether there really is a great difference of opinion or not.

SARTRE: All right. But please remember, I am talking about this life only. Of *course* we have a great difference of opinion about the next, about immortality, and God.

SOCRATES: So what am I in this life, according to your philosophy?

SARTRE: You are what you do. You are your life.

SOCRATES: And by "your life" you mean only your free, conscious choices and actions?

SARTRE: Yes. That is your being-for-itself. The "it" that you are not (and therefore can't take with you) is all being-in-itself.

SOCRATES: So if my self is only my free and *conscious* acts, then my self does not include an unconscious or subconscious part.

SARTRE: That is correct. I deny the existence of the unconscious self. I say that concept is an oxymoron, a self-contradiction. What is *un*conscious is precisely *not*-self.

SOCRATES: So there is no reservoir of hidden potentiality in me, for good or for evil, that I am not aware of.

SARTRE: Correct again. I deny any potentiality in the self.

SOCRATES: That is a strange and unusual teaching. I have no potentialities or possibilities in me that I have not yet actualized? No capabilities that I have not taken advantage of?

SARTRE: No!

SOCRATES: You are aware that almost everyone in the world would disagree with you there, I'm sure. Both psychology and common sense believe in the unconscious.

SARTRE: Yes. And I will tell you the origin of that popular superstition.

SOCRATES: I am all ears.

SARTRE: It is because they want to make excuses for themselves. For instance, a polite professor will write a polite letter of recommendation for a student of his, a student who has not yet accomplished anything significant, and the letter will say that the student has "great potential". That is simply an excuse for a loser. It is a way of lying in order to be nice, a way of denying and evading responsibility.

SOCRATES: I think I understand what you are saying, and even perhaps why you say it. Whether it is *true* or not is another question, which we will have to explore later. But I must first be sure of the first thing, that I understand your idea, before beginning the second thing, trying to find out whether it is true. So please be patient with me as I explore this idea—that "I *am* my life"—from another angle.

SARTRE: What angle?

SOCRATES: That of your own life, in concrete actuality rather than in abstract theory.

SARTRE: My life has been quite public. I also wrote an autobiography, *The Words*. I have nothing to hide.

SOCRATES: I have examined all the public data. But there is something about you that I simply do not understand. Why was it always women and not men who adored you and believed you and followed you?

SARTRE: Why do you see that as remarkable? Or even significant? What does that have to do with the meaning and truth of my ideas, as distinct from interesting personal gossip?

SOCRATES: Because this idea of yours, that "I am my life", might seem sensible to a *man*, especially a man of action, but it cannot possibly seem sensible to a woman, at least not any ordinary woman. Surely you have noticed that the first question men usually ask about someone is "What does he do?" A man tends

to identify with his work. Losing his job, or changing careers, is much more traumatic to him than to
a woman. Men identify themselves with their work
much more than women do. You don't deny that, do
you?

SARTRE: No. But perhaps that is due to either environment or heredity. Perhaps it is merely traditional
social conditioning. Or perhaps that has something
to do with physiology. In the words of a kindergarten
sex education program, "boys are fancy on the outside, girls are fancy on the inside." A man forges his
identity by his work. Both the pen and the sword are
phallic symbols.

SOCRATES: So why would a woman accept this radically masculine philosophy of yours, this identifica-
tion of your very identity with your actions?

SARTRE: A stereotypical woman would not accept it.
I was *not* understood or adored by cowherds or wet
nurses, but by women who were free, French, and
feminist.

SOCRATES: I see. The kind of woman that readers
meet in your novels and plays, and perhaps in Paris,
but rarely in the rest of the world. The kind of women
who became your mistresses, especially Simone de
Beauvoir.

SARTRE: I thought this was going to be an examination of my book, and my philosophy. Why are you
turning from examining my philosophy to examining
my private life? Is this the Last Judgment?

SOCRATES: Oh, no, not at all. It is only the *first* judgment: on your books, and your ideas. And I ask you about your life precisely to understand your philosophy. That seems fair, especially since your philosophy claims that one's being *is* one's life.

SARTRE: So how does Simone help you to understand my claim?

SOCRATES: I think I see why you admired her. Her most famous book, *The Second Sex*, is a bitter protest against everything feminine. So naturally she is called a "feminist".

SARTRE: I see: she and I are both to be judged by society's stereotypes. And you are the caretaker of the stereotypes, disguised as Platonic Ideas. So this *is* judgment rather than exploration.

SOCRATES: No, it is exploration.

SARTRE: Then your insult was out of place.

SOCRATES: But it was relevant to my exploration of the puzzle about your women. Why did French women adore you, if most women in the rest of the world would call your philosophy the most extreme example of male chauvinism since Nietzsche?

SARTRE: Are you calling Nietzsche a male chauvinist too?

SOCRATES: Perhaps that is too mild a term for the man who wrote, "Are you going to meet a woman? Then remember to bring a whip."

SARTRE: Then why do more women write doctoral dissertations in philosophy on him than on any other philosopher? And why does feminist theory, and French deconstructionism, rely on him so heavily?

SOCRATES: That is precisely what puzzles me. You French have the reputation for being decadent, and that is surely deserved—though you have no monopoly on decadence. But you also have the reputation for being supremely logical, or Cartesian: "clear and distinct ideas". Yet a "feminist" like Simone looks like a logical self-contradiction: not within the theory but between the theory and the practice. It looks as if the problem is not in the hypothesis but in the hypocrisy.

SARTRE: I demand an apology for that insult!

SOCRATES: And I cheerfully give it to you. An apology is a small price to pay for the privilege of a good insult. Especially if it is true.

SARTRE: I see. We *are* in Hell, and you are my torturer. With your tongue, not with pitchforks. For sticks and stones just break my bones, but names will really hurt me.

SOCRATES: I cannot conquer you in cleverness, Jean-Paul, nor do I claim to.

SARTRE: How supremely clever of you to say that— and thus to conquer!

SOCRATES: How supremely clever of *you* to say *that* —that thus to conquer!

SARTRE: So you always have the last word, and the trump card, in this place?

SOCRATES: No, never. Another does. But no more diversions! We must return to our serious business of investigating your philosophy by investigating your life. Would you please tell me why you think Simone stood by you, violating her own feminist principles so spectacularly, by letting you treat her so abusively all your life? I understand philosophy, but I simply do not understand women at all.

SARTRE: That is painfully evident, Socrates. Therefore, since philosophy is the thing you understand best and women are the thing you understand least, it is ridiculous for you to try to understand my philosophy by first understanding my women.

SOCRATES: I accept your syllogism as irrefutable, and so I abandon my quest. I return from your women to you, and from you to your book.

SARTRE: Finally!

SOCRATES: But I still do not understand how you can deny the very existence of the unconscious, and then call that a plus, a kind of humanism.

SARTRE: Because it is in the name of freedom, and that is man's dignity. As I wrote, **"Subjectivity . . . [is] the name we are labeled with when charges are made against us. But what do we really mean by this if not that man has a greater dignity than a stone?"**   EHE, 15–16

SOCRATES: But *no* one thinks man has no more dignity than a stone. If that is all you mean, why do you dress up a platitude in a paradox? Why say something no one denies in language no one accepts?

SARTRE: It is not a platitude. I champion freedom more radically than anyone else does. Everyone wants to give man more dignity than a stone, but I do this in a more radical way than anyone else does. As I said, **"this theory is the only one which gives man dignity, the only one which does not reduce him to an object."**

SOCRATES: But you are not the only philosopher who says man is not an object. That idea is very common. Many philosophers accept it. But they do not accept your negatives: no essence, no human nature, no design, no meaning, nothing but "absurdity". All that is what they say *robs* man of dignity rather than *giving* him dignity. And the traditional ideas about man that you reject, ideas like "the image of God" or "the king of creation"—you say these ideas *rob* man of dignity while others say they *give* man dignity.

SARTRE: That is correct.

SOCRATES: It seems you and they have very different notions of "dignity". Is that so?

SARTRE: Yes. I say human dignity consists in his transcendence of nature, and all that is associated with nature, such as potentiality (and thus the unconscious), and the womb, and stereotypical "femininity", and receptivity, and submission, and heredity. And also the cultural heredity of the human race, its past, its traditions, its inherited community or larger family. Even the relationships of family and marriage I say are dangers and threats to one's freedom. Even friendships are. See how much I sacrifice for freedom! Traditionalists see all these other things as positive, but

I see them as negative, because of their danger to freedom. Freedom is my absolute. I am indeed negative toward all these other things, but only because I must be totally positive toward freedom.

SOCRATES: But freedom itself is a minus, a negative thing, in your philosophy.

SARTRE: Only as liberation from prison is a negative thing from the jailer's viewpoint. It is a positive thing for the prisoner.

SOCRATES: And by the prison you mean nature, or being-in-itself, while by the prisoner you mean man, or being-for-itself.

SARTRE: Yes.

SOCRATES: What a shocking image for the fundamental relationship between man and nature: a jail cell! If that is so, why does everyone feel the opposite? Why do we feel that when we get out of our cities and workplace into the country and nature that we are *freed* from prison?

SARTRE: Because most men *enjoy* the irresponsibility of being imprisoned, and fear the total responsibility of being liberated. Like the prisoners in Plato's cave: they don't want to be dragged up the steep ascent into the real world.

SOCRATES: Perhaps you are more of a Platonist than you seem after all. Your image of nature as a prison reminds me very much of Plato's image of the body (*soma*) as the tomb (*sema*), or the coffin, for the soul.

SARTRE: Since we are now arguing about images, or comparing images, I must say I feel far more kinship to Machiavelli's image for the relationship between man and nature. The successful prince, he says, must by his strength of mind and will (his *virtu*) beat and coerce *fortuna*, the strumpet Fortune, which represents all the things that come to him from without, from chance or nature.

SOCRATES: First imprisonment and now rape: what wonderful images for man's fundamental relationship to nature!

SARTRE: I never claimed that life is "wonderful".

SOCRATES: Indeed you didn't. Well, you are consistent, at least. I recall all the images of nature in your writings, and of the things naturally associated with nature, like wombs: they all elicit disgust from you. For instance Roquentin's famous "nausea" at the pregnant-looking, bloated chestnut tree root, in *La Nausée*; or Mathjieu's disgust at his mistress' pregnancy in *Roads to Liberty*; or the analysis in *Being and Nothingness* of "the gooey"—soft, sticky things like spiderwebs, that seem to you to be out to entrap you, to capture your freedom, like a woman's body. I think any psychiatrist would salivate to have you as his patient. I have hardly ever met a man more terrified of women, or a psychology more limited to masculine projects: conscious, free, deliberate acts, control, maintaining one's independence, not getting caught or trapped in relationships, or families, or marriage, and finding meaning only in mastery over objects. And above all, identifying persons only with what they do and not with what they are—in fact, denying that they are anything at all. If the term "male chauvinist" does not fit you, I do not know who else in the whole history of human thought that it ever did fit.

SARTRE: Then why did women fawn over me? Have you solved that problem yet, Socrates?

SOCRATES: No. Unless they were not women at all, but anti-women, who hated or feared their own womanhood as much as you did. But that only throws back the mystery a step: why would so many women hate their own womanhood and demand to be either masculine or sexless?

SARTRE: I can't answer your question, Socrates. I think it's a bad question. You'll have to answer it yourself. Or find one of those women to enlighten you. But your answer is not here today.

SOCRATES: Perhaps it is.

SARTRE: What do you mean?

SOCRATES: Perhaps *you* are the reason. Perhaps men like you made these women feel ashamed of being women. No, I will not pursue that line of thinking here; it would take the talents of a Freud, which I do not have. Perhaps you will meet him here soon. Hmm, no, that wouldn't do either. Freud understood women not much better than you did. Let's just drop the subject.

SARTRE: That's the second time you tried to.

SOCRATES: Touché. The subject is fascinating—to men, at least. But that's why we should drop it: there are only men here, and no women. So we have no data. Neither of us is a woman.

SARTRE: And neither of us ever will be a woman, either. So we are equally foolish here.

SOCRATES: No, because one of us *listened* to women. The two highest wisdoms I ever discovered came to me through two women. One was the Delphic oracle, the prophetess (if you've read Plato's account in the *Apology*). The other was the mystic Diotima in the *Symposium*. You, on the other hand, simply never stopped talking long enough to listen, especially to women. Everyone who ever met you remarked about that.

SARTRE: Once again I ask you: Is this inquisition about me or my book?

SOCRATES: Alas, I fear I am not doing my job very well.

SARTRE: You are certainly not being very Socratic. I've been waiting all day for your famous "Socratic method" to appear. Where are your syllogisms? Where are your careful definitions and distinctions? Where are your long, tedious, multi-step linear arguments? Where is your subtle indirectness, and suggestion, and impersonal objectivity?

SOCRATES: I seem to have forgotten them. I plead guilty as charged.

SARTRE: Welcome to the human race, Mister Philosophy.

SOCRATES: Oh, I have always been there. My concern is not about my membership in that very large family, but about yours. And that is why I cannot do what I hoped a minute ago I could do, namely to simply abandon the topic of women. I cannot do that even though there is no data here, no woman. Because there *is* present here two *consequences* of that data, the footprints if not the feet. For woman is the portal through which we all fall into a family, and into the family of the human race. The origin of every family, and thus of every human, is precisely "a man *and a woman*". So to "know thyself", to examine and understand man, we must examine and understand woman. Back to work, Socrates!

SARTRE: Do you talk to yourself like that all the time?

SOCRATES: Not nearly as incessantly as you do.

SARTRE: "Back to work" then. We must examine the origin of a family, you say. But everyone knows the biological and psychological origin. We must examine the ontological origin of it. That is where my philosophy is different from most modern philosophies of woman, which are only psychological or sociological.

SOCRATES: Then let us revisit your fundamental ontological categories of being-in-itself and being-for-itself. Do these correspond to the ontological femininity and ontological masculinity, to *anima* and *animus*, or *yin* and *yang*?

SARTRE: No. *Yin* and *yang* are Platonic Ideas or Jungian archetypes.

SOCRATES: And you do not believe in Platonic Ideas or Jungian archetypes.

SARTRE: No.

SOCRATES: I understand that Platonic Ideas must go if God must go, for there if there is no divine Mind, there are no divine Ideas. But why do Jungian archetypes have to go too, if they are only in us?

SARTRE: Because they are in the "collective unconscious". I do not believe in even the individual unconscious, or the Freudian "subconscious," much less Jung's "collective unconscious". For they would render man passive and not free, not responsible. Remember, I maintain that a man's life is nothing but the sum total of his actions. Anything else would compromise his freedom. Don't you remember that part of our conversation? You've been here thousands of years; you must be getting forgetful by now.

SOCRATES: I remember quite well. You ascribe to man two attributes that traditional theology ascribes only to God: total freedom and pure actuality. So you deny receptivity and potentiality in man. I think that causes you a great difficulty when it comes to your philosophy of woman. To see this difficulty, let me begin with a psychological principle that no modern psychologist denies, I think: the principle of psychosomatic unity. Do you accept that?

SARTRE: I am not afraid to swim alone against the stream.

SOCRATES: Do you deny the psychosomatic unity then? Do you say that man is all *psyche*, or all *soma*, or two substances, like a ghost in a machine? Do you think you are a robot haunted by an angel?

SARTRE: Certainly not. Let's say I accept the psychosomatic unity—although I reserve the right to reject any particular version of it that I suspect you will foist on me.

SOCRATES: Fine. Now to our second premise. Do you deny that that which distinguishes a man from a woman on the somatic level, or the somatic dimension, includes the fact that a man has a penis while a woman has a vagina?

SARTRE: Of course not. But I do not reduce the difference between a man and a woman to that.

SOCRATES: Neither do I. But that is the most obvious difference as far as their physical organs are concerned. They are called "sex organs", after all. If you were examining some animal to find out whether it is male or female, that is what you would look at, is it not?

SARTRE: Of course.

SOCRATES: Now you also maintained that a man's being is nothing but his actions, his activities.

SARTRE: Yes.

SOCRATES: And the activity of a woman's distinctive sex organ is to receive, is it not? While that of the man's is to act, to give, to initiate, to impinge.

SARTRE: Biologically, yes.

SOCRATES: But there is my conclusion: it cannot be *merely* biological if you accept the psychosomatic unity. Any innate and essential difference in one dimension must be reflected in the other somehow.

SARTRE: So your conclusion is that there is a "feminine mind" and a "masculine mind", Platonic Forms or Jungian archetypes, "anima" and "animus".

SOCRATES: That would seem to logically follow from the three premises of the psychosomatic unity, the obvious structural and functional difference between the sex organs, and your principle that a man's life is merely the sum of his acts.

SARTRE: A *person*'s life, man *or* woman.

SOCRATES: Not quite. For if men are more active than women, they will have fuller lives. So if we accept your premises we must arrive at the conclusion that men are more human than women.

SARTRE: That is absurd.

SOCRATES: Yes it is. So one of your premises must be false. And isn't it most likely that it is the one that nearly everyone would reject, the reduction of one's life to one's acts, rather than the other two, which nearly everyone accepts?

SARTRE: If most people accept your two premises, then why don't they believe in your conclusion, those old stereotypes of yours? If they accept the psychosomatic unity and the innate physical difference in sexual organs, why don't they accept the innate difference in spirit, or mind? Why are they rightly suspicious of "the feminine mind" and "the masculine mind"?

SOCRATES: I don't think they are. I think they're rightly suspicious of artificial social constructs and role playing that many people confuse with that. *Those* are stereotypes, created by social artifice. Masculinity and femininity are archetypes, inherent in their natures.

SARTRE: I do not accept your assumption that the number of people who believe an idea is an index of how likely it is to be true. We fool ourselves all the time. It is very common.

SOCRATES: Don't you think I know that? All I said is that it *seems* more *probable* that the *very* few are wrong than that the very many are. Let's call that the Practical Principle of Minimal, Moderate Trust in Traditional, Ordinary Opinions, or PPMMTTOO. Do you believe that, at least?

SARTRE: I do—not!

SOCRATES: I see. Do you know what most people would call that "not"?

SARTRE: What?

SOCRATES: Snobbery.

SARTRE: I thought you were in the argument business, Socrates, not the name-calling business. "Snobbery"—that doesn't sound much like "syllogism". Are you forgetting who you are? "Know thyself", O philosopher!

SOCRATES: Oh, well, if it is a syllogism you want, it is a syllogism I shall give you. Major premise: One who does not believe PPMMTTOO is what men call a snob. Jean-Paul Sartre does not believe in PPMMTTOO. Therefore John-Paul Sartre is what men call a snob.

SARTRE: Surprise, surprise, you syllogize!

SOCRATES: Well, if you do not object to that conclusion about *you*, we can return to the more important question about what is true of everyone. Or perhaps you do *not* think that is more important?

SARTRE: You are a master of the velvet barb, Socrates. You must have spent some time with Machiavelli, or Oscar Wilde. Is this what you call returning to the question of "what is true for everyone"? When will you begin your return?

SOCRATES: Right now. What is true for everyone would be ontology, or metaphysics, would it not?— the division of philosophy that deals with the most universal questions of all?

SARTRE: Yes.

SOCRATES: So we should locate your philosophy of woman, and man, in the context of your ontology.

SARTRE: Yes.

SOCRATES: And the fundamental categories of your ontology are being-for-itself and being-in-itself.

SARTRE: Yes.

SOCRATES: Well, one obvious connection shows itself immediately: what you call being-in-itself seems to correspond to what is traditionally labeled the masculine, the cosmic masculine, what the Chinese call *yang*, and being-for-itself to the feminine or *yin*. Yet you reject that correspondence, don't you?

SARTRE: That depends on what you mean by the correspondence.

SOCRATES: Well, for one thing I would mean an analogy rather than an exact identity. The obvious analogy would seem to be between the masculine and being-in-itself, the realm of objects, which are identical with themselves. They are logical; they obey the law of identity. They are stiff and rigid, like triangles. Being-for-itself, on the other hand, would be the feminine, the liquid and the questionable. Is that something like what you mean?

SARTRE: Not even close. In fact, almost exactly the opposite.

SOCRATES: I am indeed surprised. Have I misunderstood being-in-itself and being-for-itself or masculinity and femininity?

SARTRE: Both, I think.

SOCRATES: I am waiting to be corrected.

SARTRE: What I mean by being-in-itself is what I think *you* mean by the cosmic archetype of the *feminine*: moving, teeming, blooming, pregnant, soft, sticky, viscous, fat, flabby, heavy, *de trop*. It has no reason to be, it just is, it is absurd. My images for it are usually soft, flowing things like knobby tree roots, or mucous, rather than hard things like triangles.

On the other hand, it is being-*for*-itself that corresponds to what your archetype would label the masculine: it is active, free, self-choosing, self-creating. Unlike you, I do not associate this with masculinity as distinct from femininity. Being-for-itself is the realm of conscious freedom by which we *all* create meaning and values, impose values on the valueless, and give meanings to our meaninglessness.

SOCRATES: I see. Or at least I think I do. But perhaps I do not. Let me put what I think I see into a syllogism again, and test it against your instruction, since you are the author.

SARTRE: I can't wait.

SOCRATES: My major premise is that you clearly and constantly idealize and love and exalt this realm of being-for-itself and impugn its other and opposite, being-in-itself. My minor premise is your admission that being-for-itself is the masculine and being-in-itself is the feminine. My conclusion is that you are the greatest male chauvinist in the history of philosophy. For all meaning and value comes from the masculine principle, according to you; the feminine is absurd and meaningless and valueless in itself, and totally dependent on the masculine to force meaning upon it.

SARTRE: No, no, that is not my point at all.

SOCRATES: Then which of my two premises is false? For the conclusion clearly follows if both are true.

SARTRE: I do not believe in *yin* and *yang*, or cosmic archetypes, or Platonic Ideas of so-called masculinity and femininity.

SOCRATES: But almost every psychologist would easily recognize these two classical sexual archetypes in your description of these two modes of being. Do you deny any connection at all, then?

SARTRE: There is some sort of connection, of course. The images I use for being-in-itself are indeed the traditional images for the cosmic feminine, or Mother

Nature, or *yin*. But this proves nothing, because only an identity between idea and idea can prove something, and this is only an identity between an image and an idea. It is not even an identity, only a popular association.

SOCRATES: But surely it is a highly suggestive connection: all those images of stickiness that entrap one's freedom, like a spider's web entrapping the free-flying fly—and it is always the female spider, never the male spider—would not any psychologist see in this a deep fear of women?

SARTRE: If so, they are bad psychologists.

SOCRATES: Even if the whole world says one thing and you say the other?

SARTRE: I refute their ideology not with my ideology but with fact: myself. Far from a fear of women, I have had many, many woman admirers, many, many mistresses, and one woman who was both an admirer and a lifelong mistress, Simone de Beauvoir.

SOCRATES: That is true. But it does not prove you have no fear of women. It is also true that you were notorious for seducing your female students.

SARTRE: I do not deny it. And it proves I have no fear of women.

SOCRATES: I think not. For you kept every one of these women at a distance. You would never even remotely consider emotional intimacy, certainly not marriage.

SARTRE: Ugh! One of the most alienating institutions ever invented!

SOCRATES: I think you can thank that alienating institution for your existence.

SARTRE: That is no inconsistency. My own existence is alienating.

SOCRATES: So you hate both.

SARTRE: So you again morph from Socrates into Freud.

SOCRATES: It is difficult to avoid it. Everyone noted how remarkable your relationships with women were. They were all either purely intellectual admirers, or purely animal mistresses. There was no union between these two things. You never had a relationship with a whole person. At least that is what most psychologists would say.

SARTRE: They would be wrong. Simone was both my admirer and my mistress.

SOCRATES: So were most of the students you seduced.

SARTRE: What is lacking, then?

SOCRATES: A whole human being.

SARTRE: What do you mean by that? Do you say the mind they admired with their minds was not a human mind? Or that the body they pleasured with their bodies was not a human body?

SOCRATES: No.

SARTRE: Then, if man is mind and body, and we have both halves here, we have a whole here. Are you saying that two halves do not make a whole?

SOCRATES: No, I am saying that two halves do not make a *human*. Most people do not recognize themselves as simply a mind plus a body. That is what Gilbert Ryle called the myth of the ghost in the machine, the haunted robot, the angel unnaturally coupled with the animal, something as unnatural as a centaur. It is not what most people mean by a man.

SARTRE: Are you arguing from the authority of the masses? I'm surprised at you, Socrates. Perhaps they are wrong. They were wrong about *you*. They thought you were an atheist, and killed you, remember? Why do you care about what most people think? Why go slumming? Why collect others' old opinions from the gutter like a rag picker picking rags?

SOCRATES: You are a true snob, Jean-Paul. But that does not prove you are wrong, any more than the fact that most people agree with me more than with you proves that I am right. So we must return to the substantive issue, your philosophy of man.

SARTRE: It's about time.

SOCRATES: Yes, it is. It's much harder than most people think to keep focused on an issue. Let us resolve to explore now your claim that a man is nothing but his life, his acts.

SARTRE: Explore away, Socrates. But beware of the scorpions.

7

Am I My Life?

EHE, 32 SARTRE: I say that **"Man is nothing else than . . . the ensemble of his acts, nothing else than his life."**

SOCRATES: So you deny that there is *potentiality* in man, as classical Christian theology denies that there is potentiality in God?

SARTRE: Not in that sense, no. For the concept of God is the concept of an unchanging being. Man obviously changes. And in the classical conception, potentiality is what you have to have if you are going to change.

SOCRATES: Then what do you mean when you say man is only all his acts, and not anything potential?

SARTRE: Exactly what I say. Man is only all the things he has done. These are acts in time, of course. But he is *not* what he *could* have been or what he *should* have been or what he *might* have been. He is only what he has made himself to be.

SOCRATES: Let me try to understand this rather severely abstract, metaphysical teaching of yours by exploring some of the more concrete consequences of

it. For one thing, you deny the existence of any unconscious mind, or unconscious self, don't you?

SARTRE: I do.

SOCRATES: And that seems connected to your denial
of the feminine, for the unconscious is something like
the feminine in ourselves.

SARTRE: If you insist on those archetypes. I would
prefer to be more conceptually precise and call it "the
other in ourselves".

SOCRATES: And as soon as you say that, everyone
who has read your unforgettable play *No Exit* must
be thinking of your most striking line, its "point"
at the end that **"Hell is the others."** What do you
think a psychologist would make of that sentence?

SARTRE: Are you psychoanalyzing me or analyzing
my book?

SOCRATES: Either of those two things may be a useful means to the other, I think.

SARTRE: What justifies you in playing the psychologist?

SOCRATES: When a man says that the sky is blue, we
are not justified in playing the psychologist and seeking a psychological explanation for his belief—for instance, saying that he thinks that because his mother
dropped him on his head when he was a baby. But
what about when he says the sky is yellow?

SARTRE: In other words, you are now playing psychologist because you believe I am evidently insane?

SOCRATES: Almost. For instance, your denial of the very existence of any unconscious mind is so strange —there is hardly a single psychologist in the world who would agree with you there—that it would seem to call for a psychological explanation.

SARTRE: Again you are *assuming* the rightness of bourgeois common sense. That is not like you, Socrates. In fact, I think you are not Socrates at all, but a Socrates impersonator.

SOCRATES: I am not assuming that bourgeois common sense is right. Nor do I confine myself to the bourgeoisie, for that is not the whole human race but only a portion of it: that portion which you, like Marx, seem to assume is always wrong.

SARTRE: Enough of this badinage! What logically follows from all you have said about the truth or falsity of my idea that a man is his acts? If every psychologist in the world disbelieves it, does it follow that it is false?

SOCRATES: No, but it follows that you cannot expect your idea to be credible to many.

SARTRE: Ah, but it is. I have many admirers.

SOCRATES: You *had* many admirers. You will find this place quite different.

SARTRE: Oh. And just where is "this place", anyway? I don't recall seeing it on any of the maps they gave us in geography.

SOCRATES: Voltaire joked that the typical medieval French peasant knew more about the geography of

Heaven and Hell than about the geography of France.
He meant it as an insult, but he should have meant
it as a compliment. For wherever Voltaire is now, he
is not in France. And neither are you.

But I am still puzzled about all those admirers you
had there. I especially wonder why almost all your admirers were women. And why you never had a lasting male friend. And why women could accept a psychology that seems to deny all that is distinctively or
typically feminine.

SARTRE: You mean to return to your old stereotype?

SOCRATES: No, I mean to return to your metaphysical category of potentiality.

SARTRE: But it is only your old stereotype that asso-
ciates potentiality with femininity.

SOCRATES: It is not only an old stereotype. It is data.
It is physical data, in fact.

SARTRE: Impossible. Metaphysics is not physics.

SOCRATES: May I try to show you the impossible?

SARTRE: Go ahead.

SOCRATES: Is it a physical fact that a woman has a
womb?

SARTRE: Of course.

SOCRATES: And that a womb has the power to grow,
or nurture, or bring forth, a baby?

SARTRE: Of course.

SOCRATES: And is it a physical fact that a human baby,
born or unborn, has a power that no animal baby has,

namely the potentiality, or power, to become a human adult and to perform distinctively human acts like reasoning?

SARTRE: I do not deny that a human baby *will* in fact become a human adult, but I deny that there is in it *now* some mysterious, invisible principle, or force, or power that you call "potentiality".

SOCRATES: Whether you call it "potentiality" or not, do you deny that there is *something* in that human infant that is not in the infant of any other species even though it is not yet manifesting itself?

SARTRE: Even if I admit such a *physical* power—a genetic structure, for instance—that is not *metaphysical* potentiality.

SOCRATES: Do you then deny all relation between the physical and the metaphysical?

SARTRE: I do! I deny your way of philosophizing, which was to try to rise from the physical to the metaphysical by means of some analogy. That led to either Plato's way of doing metaphysics, which culminated in mysticism, or Aristotle's way, which culminated in bad medieval science.

SOCRATES: But you *do* do metaphysics.

SARTRE: Oh, yes.

SOCRATES: Then what door do *you* use to enter the house of metaphysics?

SARTRE: The modern door, the Cartesian door. As I wrote, "**There can be no other truth to take off from than this:** *I think, therefore I exist.* **There we**

EHE, 36

have the absolute truth of consciousness becoming aware of itself . . . outside the Cartesian *cogito* all views are only probable."

You see, once you grant that man is partly a piece of nature, partly determined by nature, by *his* nature, by his essence, by his potentiality—once you go back to the pre-modern philosophy and the analogy between the physical and the metaphysical—once you do that, or to the extent that you do that, you take away his freedom and responsibility. Man becomes then only minimally responsible for himself because he is largely passive, receptive, potential, determined.

I say, on the other hand, that the self is totally act, and thus totally responsible and totally free. And I say that **"this theory is the only one which gives man dignity . . . [and] does not reduce him to an object."**

EHE, 37

SOCRATES: Do you claim that man was *not* given dignity by philosophies like Platonism or Hinduism, in which he is said to be a kind of god in disguise? Or in Christianity, in which he is said to be a child of God, created in God's image and destined to participate in the very life of God forever? Or even in secular humanism, where he is said to be hero of the cosmos, having evolved by the incredible luck of blind chance from the primordial slime, and has now learned to understand and master the very nature that brought him into being after fifteen billion years? Do you see no alternative versions of human dignity in these philosophies, but only in your own? Do you say that all those psychologists who believe in the existence of the unconscious, or the "collective unconscious", or in "human potentiality", have sacrificed human dignity?

SARTRE: That is precisely what I claim. They have compromised it, at least. Mine is the only philosophy that gives man no excuses at all, not even something like "I'm not responsible for having a hot temper, since I didn't choose my own genetic makeup."

SOCRATES: It would be interesting to explore how your view sits with homosexuals. It sounds suspiciously like what their opponents are saying about them, that their biological predisposition does not count.

SARTRE: If that means that they are nothing but their behavior, I agree with it. That is true for all of us.

SOCRATES: Come to think of it, that is exactly what *they* usually say: "If you reject my behavior, you reject me. I am my behavior." But we shouldn't let ourselves be diverted from our general principle. You say that each of us is totally responsible for everything that he is, is that correct?

SARTRE: Yes.

SOCRATES: Including that incredibly ugly face?

SARTRE: Indeed! If I call it "mine", I claim responsibility for it. It is not the face of Fate, it is the face of Jean-Paul Sartre.

SOCRATES: And do you claim that the ugliness of your face has nothing to do with the ugliness of your soul?

SARTRE: Of course not. This ugly face can express an ugly mood or a happy one, just as yours can.

SOCRATES: But the face you were born with, the instrument you use to express these different states of soul—do you take responsibility for that too? For instance, that your eyes are large and round and staring, like a frog's?

SARTRE: Indeed I do. As I said, that is *my* face. And if you know what's good for you, Socrates, you won't push that analogy between the physical and the metaphysical very much. For I think that in the entire history of mankind there have never been two philosophers who have been as ugly as we two. Tell me, please, how many times have you been called something like "frog face"?

SOCRATES: Too many. In fact, I am even uglier than you; my whole body, and not just my face, is lumpish and froggy.

SARTRE: Then you too are a dualist, like me. You *contrast* body and soul.

SOCRATES: I used to think in those Cartesian terms, as you do. It was from me that Plato got the idea that your self is simply your soul, and not your body. That's why I used to say that "no evil can happen to a good man, in this world or in the next"—an idea that my culture found as absurd as *your* culture found your idea that we are wholly responsible for ourselves and that there are no accidents in the realm of the self.

SARTRE: You say you *used* to think that way. Do you now say you were wrong?

SOCRATES: Partly. I think I was wrong in two ways. First, about the body. Obviously, others can do evil to my body. And my body is part of myself. So evil men *can* harm good men. I was wrong in thinking that my body was simply my tomb, or my prison house, and not part of myself. And I also made a second mistake. I should have had the common sense to see this distinction: I was right in thinking that no evil can be *forced* on a good man. But even if the self is only the soul and not the body, someone else can make it *harder* for me to be wise and good and happy, for instance by torturing me or by deceiving me.

SARTRE: So you suddenly changed your mind and your philosophy after you died?

SOCRATES: Not so suddenly. I was moving toward it while I lived. There was an incident in my life which taught me to question my sharp dualism between body and soul, and it stemmed from my ugly face. I think you would be interested in hearing this story.

SARTRE: I think I have no choice.

SOCRATES: Are you saying that you have no freedom and no responsibility? So *you* have suddenly changed your mind and your philosophy after death? Sorry, that was a cheap shot. I will just tell you my story.

A famous Sophist from another city was visiting Athens. He had never met me and had no idea what I looked like. He was a physiognomist: he claimed to be a practitioner of the art of reading a man's character from his face. I did not think this art was possible, for you can't tell a prisoner's character from the architecture of his prison cell.

My friends decided to play a trick on him to show him the foolishness of his claim. They brought me to this Sophist, without telling him who I was, and asked him to read my character from my face. This is what he told me: "Sir, you are a bully and a war-monger. You are also arrogant and proud. Finally, you are a sensualist and self-indulgent."

At this, my friends all laughed, for I had the reputation, among them at least, for being a peaceful, humble, and temperate man. However, I did not laugh. Rather, I turned to the Sophist and said, "Sir, I did not believe in your art until now. But you have convinced me that you can indeed read a man's character in his face. For these are exactly the three vices against which I have to struggle every day."

SARTRE: So now you think a man is his face as well as his soul?

SOCRATES: I think that his beauty or ugliness of soul shines through his face and transforms it. Take the two of us here. We are both short, stubby, and frog-faced. But our similar faces speak dissimilar words. You almost never smile, and when you do, the smile looks twisted and unnatural. But I am always on the brink of making a joke, even when speaking of serious matters. Your eyes dart nervously about. But my eyes are quiet and withdrawn even when I am searching for some objective truth. And you always seem to be talking to yourself even when you are listening to me. But I am always listening, even when I am speaking.

SARTRE: What's your point, Socrates? That you are a saint and I am a sinner? That you are privileged and happy and secure in this place, while I am not? That I have a nervous energy that you fear and dislike? Is this supposed to be a proof of your personal superiority?

SOCRATES: What a strange misinterpretation! Not at all. I am trying to illustrate my general point, about my dualism of body and soul, with specific examples. I found only two at hand: myself and you. My point is only that bodies and souls are not so independent as I had thought. On this point, I thought I was admitting that you were right and I was wrong. But apparently I failed to deliver this compliment, or else you failed to receive it.

SARTRE: You forget, Socrates, that I deny that a man can receive *anything* without losing some of his freedom.

SOCRATES: Even a compliment?

SARTRE: Especially a compliment. An insult does far less harm to one's freedom. The Nazis insulted us, during the War, during the Resistance, but that did not diminish our freedom. It increased it. Because we were threatened with death every moment, every choice took on the glare of that light, a step on the brink, a deliberate declaration of principle.

SOCRATES: I see your point. You need not go on with your self-aggrandizing lies about your heroism.

SARTRE: What do you mean by that slander?

SOCRATES: You know very well that all you did for the Resistance was to sit at a table and write. Your friends took all the risks, and suffered all the imprisonments and tortures. Your "we" is a bit disingenuous. You see, deception is no longer possible in this place.

SARTRE: I knew it. I am in Hell.

SOCRATES: I will not be distracted again! We are speaking of far more momentous things than your little lies. We are speaking of your identity, of every man's identity, of whether that is double or single.

SARTRE: And are you saying that you had thought it was single and now think it is double? That when you were alive you thought a man was only his soul and now you think he is also his body?

SOCRATES: No, I am saying almost the opposite: that when I was alive I sharply separated soul and body, but now I see their oneness.

SARTRE: How can that be? What bridges the gap? If by "soul" you mean "mind", how do you overcome the total gap between these two "clear and distinct ideas" of Descartes? A mind has consciousness and no extension in space, while a body has extension in space and no consciousness. How can one be an analogy or an image for the other? How can your face show your soul? What does a soul look like? Is it square, or red, or angular?

SOCRATES: If I had known as much philosophy then as I know now, I would have answered as Wittgenstein did. He said that the best image for a human soul is a human body.

SARTRE: I thought we were supposed to be examining my philosophy here, not yours.

SOCRATES: We are. I am using mine only to expose yours, by comparison. At least that is what I am attempting to do.

SARTRE: Well, all this talk about body and soul does not affect my philosophy at all. *That* dualism is not the same as mine. Mine is between act and potency, yours is between spirit and matter, or soul and body. I do not deny that my body is part of myself, as you used to do. I deny that my *potentiality* is part of myself. I say that I am the sum of my acts. You see, even within your "soul", or "spirit", you still believe in potencies. For instance, you and your successors Plato and Aristotle believed in "virtues" and "vices", and you thought of these as moral and immoral "habits", and you thought of "habits" as positive tendencies to act in certain ways, active potencies, so to speak. And you thought of a man's "character" as the sum of these "virtuous" and "vicious" "habits". Isn't that right?

SOCRATES: I think that's right, yes.

SARTRE: Well, I think that's wrong, no.

SOCRATES: Because you say a man's being is simply his life, his acts?

SARTRE: Yes.

SOCRATES: What, exactly, do you mean by that? Do you mean that these two are co-terminous, co-extensive, that there is no more in the one than in the other?

SARTRE: That is exactly what I mean.

SOCRATES: Do you say that most people believe this?

SARTRE: No, most do not. I am trying to enlighten them, to do *your* thing to them, Socrates: "know thyself."

SOCRATES: Those who deny it, what do they mean?

SARTRE: What do you mean, "What do they mean?"

SOCRATES: Do they say that there is more in my being than in my life, or that there is more in my life than in my being? Those are the only two ways to deny it, logically, isn't that right?

SARTRE: Yes. Logically, those are the only two ways to deny it.

SOCRATES: And do those who deny it usually say that there is more in my life than in my being?

SARTRE: No, that would be absurd. How could it be *my* life without *my* being being in it somehow?

SOCRATES: So they say that there is more in one's being than in one's life.

SARTRE: Yes.

SOCRATES: And what do you think they mean by that?

SARTRE: Two things, I think: one metaphysical and the other ethical. And the two are connected. The metaphysical claim is that I am some mysterious, hidden bunch of potentialities over and above my actual choices; something created not by me but by nature, or by God, or by Fate, or by other people; something that is me but which is not me, for I am not responsible for it. And that disclaimer of responsibility for what they are is the second thing they mean. In fact, that is their real point, or "bottom line". That is the *point* of the point: the ethical point about responsibility is the point of the metaphysical point about being. Nietzsche was right: to understand a philosopher's metaphysics, look at the ethics it leads to.

SOCRATES: So you argue against this other philosophy—the traditional or commonsensical one that says that there is more in my being than in my life —you argue against it in the reverse order, so to speak, from ethics to metaphysics instead of from metaphysics to ethics: in order to deny its disclaimer of responsibility, you believe you have to deny its notion of potentialities in the self.

SARTRE: Yes. That is my reasoning. It does not move, like yours, from metaphysics to ethics but from ethics to metaphysics. My premise is the ethical one: that I am totally responsible for being what I am.

SOCRATES: *All* that you are? Including your ugliness of face?

SARTRE: Yes. I do not claim that I am something potentially beautiful but that the actualization of this beauty has been aborted by some accident or chance that I could do nothing about. I do not claim that I am a plant that *would* have blossomed into a beautiful flower because it already had within itself some invisible potentiality to beauty, something real yet not actually real, something which depended on external accidental conditions to actualize it. I will have none of these excuses! Rather, I claim that I create my own self and am as wholly responsible for it as God would be for the universe if He had created it.

SOCRATES: But you make yourself out of certain pre-existing materials, while God supposedly created the universe out of nothing, with no limitations or parameters. Doesn't that difference between you and God make your responsibility less than total?

SARTRE: No. For I do not make myself out of pre-existing materials. I create my meaning, my identity, my values, out of nothing, like God, not out of something, like a carpenter creating a table out of wood. *Who I am* is not determined by my body or my fate or my friends. I am the master of my fate, I am the captain of my soul. I am my life.

SOCRATES: —and *no more than* your life.

SARTRE: Right.

SOCRATES: So if you are no more than your life, you cannot transcend it, or withdraw from it, or take a position toward it, as you take a position toward another, toward an object.

SARTRE: Exactly. My life is not an "other" to me, as it is to you. It is *me*.

SOCRATES: So you cannot know it or judge it as an object.

SARTRE: You cannot.

SOCRATES: So "know thyself" is impossible.

SARTRE: I realize this must sound shocking to you, Socrates, but your whole life's quest is a wild goose chase. You can never catch the goose because you *are* the goose.

SOCRATES: I see.

SARTRE: Do you, really?

SOCRATES: I think so. Your argument makes sense. I cannot know myself because the knower must transcend the known, and I cannot transcend myself.

SARTRE: It's not that simple. In one way, you *always* transcend yourself, but in another way you never do. I do admit a "transcendence of the ego". . . .

SOCRATES: I have read that passage in *Being and Nothingness*, but I'd rather not go into it here, because it is very difficult. Let's just look at the way we *can't* transcend ourselves. Because that's your reason for saying that my being is only my life. Do you think you could explain your argument to me in a way I could understand?

SARTRE: I'll try. Let's begin with a logical assumption: that *the knowledge of any object must transcend that object, it cannot be one of the parts of that object.* For if it *were* only a *part* of that object, then it could not know the *whole* object. If, on the other hand, it does know the whole object, then it has to transcend that object, it has to be outside that object, to use a spatial metaphor, looking down on it from above or outside. For if it were inside the object, it would be only one of the parts of that object.

To make the same point in a different way: If I were to know the whole universe, I would have to know my act of knowing the whole universe, because that act is part of the universe. But then I would also have to know my act of knowing my act of knowing, otherwise I would not know the whole. And that new act would create a new universe, so to speak, which could be wholly known only by an act-of-knowing which would create a new and larger universe, one with one additional act in it. And so on, forever.

And thus "know thyself" as an object is in principle impossible. Your life's quest is a useless passion, Socrates, like man himself.

SOCRATES: What an absolutely brilliant argument! Stunning in its simplicity!

SARTRE: But . . . ?

SOCRATES: What do you mean, "But . . . "?

SARTRE: With you there's always a big but.

SOCRATES: Not on my mind. I am quite convinced by your argument, and I think you are simply right.

SARTRE: So you now abandon your life's quest to "know thyself"?

SOCRATES: No, I do not think that follows at all.

SARTRE: Why? It certainly seems to follow from my argument.

SOCRATES: Perhaps you are right about the individual self. But my quest was not for that. It was for 'human nature,' the common human essence that your Nominalism denies.

SARTRE: But as far as the individual self is concerned, do you admit that "know thyself" is absurd?

SOCRATES: I admit it is a paradox. But I do not think it is absurd. I think it is something more like a Zen *koan*, a puzzle which cannot, in principle, be solved, but which has the side effect of triggering "Enlightenment". One could interpret the moral law this way —the Ten Commandments or Kant's Categorical Imperative—for no man can obey it perfectly and yet all men are obligated to obey it perfectly. It is something useful, even necessary, for us even though we find it impossible of fulfillment. I think they call this kind of thing *upaya* in India: a kind of creative trick. Something like the carrot on the stick held in front of the horse on the treadmill.

So even if we can never catch the wild goose, the wild goose chase might be far from absurd. It might take us for a wonderful flight through the sky. For look at the consequences of that wild goose chase. It is not only *my* quest, but that of all of mankind, or at least that part of it that you call Western civilization, ever since we Greeks got you embarked on that quest. You yourself ride a wave from that swell, Jean-Paul. If I had not set mankind on this "impossible quest", you would never have written your books.

SARTRE: I did not realize how close to you I was, Socrates. And how tricky. Perhaps we were both embarked upon an *upaya* in our philosophizing.

SOCRATES: If so, it was not I who was the trickster, but the god.

SARTRE: God? What god? (I fear our agreement is going to be very short-lived.)

SOCRATES: The god of the Delphic oracle, over whose temple this command was inscribed: "know thyself" (*gnothi seauton*). The god who gave me my *koan*: that no one in the world was wiser than Socrates, who had no wisdom at all. It was this god, whoever he was, who was the trickster, for his puzzle was my carrot on my stick. It set me upon a lifelong quest for a man wiser than myself, and for this quest I developed the art of logical cross-examination that became the Socratic method, and the basis for Plato's philosophy and Aristotle's logic. See how tricky the god was: in giving Socrates this riddle, he was using the Socratic method on Socrates in order to prod Socrates to develop the Socratic method in order to solve the god's riddle!

SARTRE: But that's just the kind of thing I want to deny. You are ascribing responsibility for your becoming a philosopher to "the god". But it was your own quest, your own response to the god's riddle, and thus your own responsibility. Surely other people would have responded to the same riddle in different ways.

SOCRATES: That's true.

SARTRE: And even if it was an oracle of a god, it was your interpretation of the oracle that determined its meaning for you. I wrote, **"The existentialist does not think that man is going to help himself by finding in the world some omen by which to orient himself. Because he thinks that man will interpret the omen to suit himself."** Just as you are

EHE, 23

responsible for your life, you are also responsible for your interpretations, your beliefs, your thoughts.

SOCRATES: There is something to that, certainly. Even the Christians agree. Saint Paul told them to "take every thought captive to Christ". Perhaps you are not as far as you think you are from their epistemology.

SARTRE: No, I remain very far from it. I would distinguish sharply the two parts of that saying. The first part is right: the "taking", the active choice regarding your thinking. The second part is not: the giving, the giving of your very thoughts to the god, to Christ. And even more important is a third, unstated part: the *receiving* that is assumed in their (and your) belief in "objective" truth. I deny that assumption, not because I am a skeptic—I'm not—but because I'm a humanist, and I find it demeaning to human dignity to make the assumption that the mind, or the self, is passive to truth, like a camera to light.

SOCRATES: And so you deny that fundamental common sense definition of truth, don't you, which Aristotle defined as conformity to reality, or "thinking and saying of what is that it is, and of what is not that it is not"?

SARTRE: I do.

SOCRATES: Why?

SARTRE: Because nothing comes *to* being-for-itself. Things come only *to* being-in-itself. Being-for-itself is free and active and creative. It is the source of meaning and values. Being-in-itself is not. Rocks don't tell my soul my meaning. And neither do gods, even if there were gods. And neither do other people.

SOCRATES: And why do you believe *that*?

SARTRE: Because if I do, then I am free and responsible, and I can never blame anyone else for what I am. And if I don't, then I'm *not* free and responsible, and I *can* blame others for what I am.

SOCRATES: Suppose another man, wholly unknown to you, sneaks up behind you and kills you. Is he not responsible for what you are: a corpse? Can you not blame him for his act? Would you blame yourself instead? Are all murders suicides?

SARTRE: I know that sounds absurd to you, but my answer is yes. You see, that is why I say that my being is nothing but my life, my acts, my choices. It is my desire to give man total freedom and responsibility. You yourself, Socrates, are what you are now not because of something the god did to you, but because of something you did to him: because of your faith in the god, and because of the way you chose to interpret the oracle. You can't blame the god for that.

SOCRATES: I did not ever blame a god for anything. What I did, however, was to praise and thank the god for something.

SARTRE: Oh, how pious of you! But how irrational! You can receive good things but not bad? You take credit for all the bad and the god takes credit for all the good? That is not only psychologically pathological, but logically inconsistent. The two things are in the same metaphysical boat.

SOCRATES: I see. So if I cannot ever blame anyone but myself, then I also cannot ever praise or thank anyone but myself.

SARTRE: That is correct.

SOCRATES: Then you have made impossible the one thing every single sage, saint, poet, moralist, humanist, mystic, and even ordinary fairly happy man, whether ancient or modern, Western or Eastern, has declared to be a *sine qua non* of both wisdom and happiness.

SARTRE: What?

SOCRATES: *Gratitude.*

SARTRE: If I am an atheist, that must be my corollary. Remember, I described my whole philosophy as an attempt to draw out all the logical consequences of atheism.

SOCRATES: But this cuts even deeper than your atheism, I think. For an atheist may still feel gratitude, and admire it, and affirm it, even if he does not believe that God is its true object, and even if he therefore has a great difficulty finding anyone to be grateful to for existence itself. Such a man is to be pitied for his philosophy, but commended for his gratitude. An ungrateful theist, on the other hand, who is arrogant and self-centered, is to be commended for his philosophy but pitied for his lack of gratitude. So what shall we say of the ungrateful atheist who is not vexed at having no God to thank for existence? That he is not to be commended for anything, but only to be pitied. But you will not agree with this judgment of all the saints and sages about gratitude, do you?

SARTRE: No.

SOCRATES: You will not even agree with the Buddhists, who say they are atheists, but value gratitude?

SARTRE: That is correct, Socrates. Even your wording is exactly right. It is not that I *cannot* do it, that my hands are tied and I am not free. It is that I *will* not do it.

SOCRATES: And the reason you will not do it is that you cannot do it without abandoning some fundamental foundation stone of your whole philosophy, isn't that right?

SARTRE: Yes.

SOCRATES: So that foundation stone must be something deeper than atheism then.

SARTRE: You are right. God's existence is ultimately irrelevant to me. Even if He did exist, I would maintain my philosophy, like Ivan Karamazov, as he says, "even if I'm wrong". Ivan says that because he is honorable, and free, and will not bow, and submit, and surrender, like a Muslim. He will not be a collaborator even though he loses. He will not buy God's ticket.

SOCRATES: Even if he is wrong? Why?

SARTRE: Because it is God's ticket, not his.

SOCRATES: So you judge the theist's life as dishonest and dishonorable, as well as wrong?

SARTRE: I have said that I will not judge another man's life, only my own.

SOCRATES: Oh, so you *do* judge your own?

SARTRE: Of course.

SOCRATES: Then you *can* judge your own. For what you do do, you can do.

SARTRE: Yes.

SOCRATES: Then you must be wrong about your being not transcending your life.

SARTRE: How does that follow?

SOCRATES: The judge must transcend the parties judged, must he not? If a hundred accused prisoners are to be judged, one of them cannot be the judge.

SARTRE: True.

SOCRATES: And you say you can judge your own life.

SARTRE: I do.

SOCRATES: Then you must transcend your life.

SARTRE: I spoke colloquially. In the precise, technical sense, I cannot judge my own life.

SOCRATES: So you are a skeptic.

SARTRE: If that is your preferred label. What am I to do with it now, find some corner called Skepticism and go there to sit and sulk in it?

SOCRATES: Not if you are consistent with your philosophy. What you are to do is to act, and blame not me but yourself for the label, if it fits, if you sewed it onto your own lips.

SARTRE: What do you mean, "sewed it onto your own lips"?

SOCRATES: Only the old argument against skepticism that Aristotle first used on Protagoras: that if you open your lips and utter a declarative sentence that you claim is true, then you are not a skeptic.

SARTRE: Go through that argument for me, please.

SOCRATES: Gladly. "Skepticism" means "We cannot know what is true." And thus "Skepticism is true" means "It is true that we cannot know what is true." And that, in turn—that "it is true that we cannot know what is true"—means "*I know* it is true that we cannot know what is true." And *that* is logically self-contradictory. And what is logically self-contradictory is necessarily false. And what is *necessarily* false, is false. Therefore skepticism is false.

SARTRE: Your formal logic does not touch the meat of my argument. It is like a label used by a butcher to mask the meat.

SOCRATES: What then is the "meat"?

SARTRE: It is not simply a generic logical skepticism. That is indeed self-contradictory, as you have shown. I am not a generic skeptic. I am skeptical of the superstition that there is some hidden treasure of potentiality in the self, like a dragon's hoard. I am suspicious of the comforting and edifying bourgeoise idea that the most boring and worthless person in the world is really a potential little god or goddess because there is some well of invisible potentiality there within him, like a seed, and if only the sun of fortune had smiled

on him, if only some god or Fate had given him special
treatment, he would have blossomed into such beautiful fruit that the world would lavish praise and gratitude upon him. What nonsense! Literally non-sense;
for it is logically self-contradictory to say that there
actually is something non-actual, something *potential*.
It is saying that the potential is actual. Only blind
and bland banality, only wimpy and weepy wishful
thinking could produce such nonsense.

And then comes the coup de grace: that after death
this loser, this stinker, this nothing, is not what we see
plainly in front of us, dirt and worms and decay, but
becomes a little god! The plant is then finally watered
by divine grace (why not earlier?) and washed clean
of all his evils and follies (as if someone else could do
that!) and brought into the presence of Omniscience,
the unavoidable light that pierces him through like
the sun through dust, so that he is now both a perfect being-for-itself and a perfect being-in-itself, like
God. No, I do not believe that nonsense. I do not
believe it is even believable. I think believers only
believe they believe it. They think they are believing
it but they are really believing in their own beliefs.
It is just an escape from responsibility, from the fact
that each of us is solely and wholly responsible for
his own life.

SOCRATES: I see.

SARTRE: Is that all you can answer?

SOCRATES: For now, yes. But you will eventually be
answered much more adequately than you can be now.

SARTRE: What do you mean?

SOCRATES: I mean that you are going to be very surprised.

SARTRE: Give me an argument, Socrates, not a threat. "Surprise" is only another word for "threat".

SOCRATES: It is I who am surprised by *that* definition of "surprise". I wonder what sort of birthday parties or Christmases *you* had. Well, I will give you an argument. Another will give you the surprise.

There is no contradiction in saying that a potentiality is actually present, for that is *not* to say that it is actually present *as an actuality*. That would indeed be self-contradictory and meaningless, as you say. But to say that an acorn actually already has the potentiality to become an oak tree in the future while a tulip bulb does not have that potentiality, is not self-contradictory or meaningless at all.

SARTRE: The metaphysics is not fundamental, Socrates. The morality is.

SOCRATES: I agree. Therefore let us examine that.

8

Responsibility

SOCRATES: We should now more carefully examine your challenging notion that we are each totally and solely responsible for our own lives.

SARTRE: Oh.

SOCRATES: You sound surprised already.

SARTRE: I am pleased. I thought your idealism would be so shocked by my low view of man, that you would spend more time attacking my negative ideas instead of looking at my positive one.

SOCRATES: Why would I do that?

SARTRE: To win the argument, of course.

SOCRATES: But I have no need or desire to win, and certainly none for you to lose. Even on earth I had no such desire, though others did, and consequently misunderstood me. But here—

SARTRE: All right, get on with it, please. What *about* my doctrine of total responsibility?

SOCRATES: I want to test a suspicion of mine.

SARTRE: Ah, I knew it. Here comes the dark stuff.

SOCRATES: The suspicion is this: that it is only a striking way of wording a truth that many others have professed, though seldom lived up to. One sage put the idea this way: "Whenever the time comes to make excuses, the time has come to do the thing you are making excuses for not doing."

SARTRE: In other words, the idea that people are far too quick to make excuses and pass the buck; that they do not live up to their own standards; that they take responsibility for only, let's say, one tenth of their lives, while they should take responsibility for nine tenths.

SOCRATES: Something like that, yes.

SARTRE: No, it is more than that. That is a common idea.

SOCRATES: God forbid your ideas should be common. People would start calling you "bourgeoise"!

SARTRE: Oh, so you are capable of sarcasm after all.

SOCRATES: I have that potentiality, whether you believe in it or not. But what I am searching for now is a definition. What do you mean by total responsibility?

SARTRE: Not just that people make excuses and don't live up to their philosophy, but that their philosophy is wrong.

SOCRATES: So it seems that, as usual, your point is as unusual as it seems.

SARTRE: Yes. I take responsibility for all my words.

SOCRATES: You poor man! That is an enormous pile to carry on your shoulders. For instance, the following passage from your book:

EHE,
54–56

There are no *accidents* in life. . . . If I am mobilized in a war, this war is *my* war; it is in my image and I deserve it. I deserve it first because I could always get out of it by suicide or by desertion. . . . For lack of getting out of it, I have *chosen* it. This can be due to inertia, to cowardice in the face of public opinion, or because I prefer certain other values to the value of the refusal to join in the war (the good opinion of my relatives, the honor of my family, etc.). Any way you look at it, it is a matter of a choice. This choice will be repeated later on again and again without a break until the end of the war. Therefore we must agree with the statement of J. Romains, "In war there are no innocent victims."

. . . But in addition the war is *mine* by the sole fact that it arises in a situation which I cause to be and that I can discover it there only by engaging myself for or against it. . . .

Finally . . . each person is an absolute upsurge at an absolute date and is perfectly unthinkable at another date. It is therefore a waste of time to ask what I would have been if this war had not broken out, for I have chosen myself as one of the possible meanings of the epoch which imperceptibly led to war. I am not distinct from this same epoch; I could not be transported to another epoch with-

out contradiction. Thus *I am* this war. . . . we have the war we deserve. Thus, totally free, undistinguishable from the period for which I have chosen to be the meaning, as profoundly responsible for the war as if I myself had declared it . . . I must be without remorse or regrets as I am without excuse; for from the instant of my upsurge into being, I carry the weight of the world by myself alone without anything or any person being able to lighten it.

You realize, of course, that on the face of it that this seems not only false but utterly ridiculous, don't you? Are you just being deliberately provocative, or perhaps exaggerating or misleading just to get the reader's attention and engagement? Do you literally mean all that, in the ordinary sense of the words you use?

SARTRE: Are you being sarcastic again?

SOCRATES: Not at all.

SARTRE: Hmm. . . . That "not at all" may itself be sarcasm. But I will assume that it is not, so I will say, as plainly and literally as you usually do, that I mean every word. I choose my words with care.

SOCRATES: Just *when* did you write these words?

SARTRE: During the War, during the German Occupation.

SOCRATES: And where were you then?

SARTRE: In Paris. Why do you find that significant?

SOCRATES: Did those in Paris who read your words believe them, or not?

SARTRE: Some did, some did not.

SOCRATES: Were you ever in one of Hitler's death camps?

SARTRE: You know I was not.

SOCRATES: Too bad. It would have been very interesting to observe you preaching this philosophy to the Jews in Auschwitz waiting in line to enter the gas chamber.

SARTRE: What's your question, Socrates? Are you getting sarcastic again, or are you examining my book?

SOCRATES: We are examining *what you mean* in your book.

SARTRE: So what's your question?

SOCRATES: How would a Jew in Auschwitz act differently if he accepted your philosophy, if he believed that "he has chosen this war", that "there are no innocent victims", and therefore that he is not an innocent victim of Hitler's genocide? Would he feel guilty for his own death? Would he identify his martyrdom with suicide? Would he accept his slaughter, and that of six million of his people, as something they all deserved, and even chose?

SARTRE: He would take responsibility for it—not by feeling guilty but by becoming active instead of passive.

SOCRATES: And what would that mean? Fighting for Germany, since Germany started the action?

SARTRE: Now you *are* being sarcastic, Socrates. You know I mean no such thing.

SOCRATES: But that is what your *words* seem to mean, and you just told me that you meant all your words literally, in the ordinary sense. And you yourself applied your principles to this specific example, so you cannot escape responsibility for their consequences. So what *would* you say to a Jew in Auschwitz to explain to him that "in war there are no innocent victims"?

SARTRE: The passage I quoted gives you not just one but three answers to that question, Socrates. Shall I go over them again?

SOCRATES: Please do. I must have missed them. I am very old, you know. And could you do it briefly and clearly, please? Remember your audience. They do not have the leisure for subtlety. They are waiting in line outside the gas chamber, and it is moving quite fast.

SARTRE: First, there are no accidents. You always have choices, alternatives, at least the choice of suicide or not. Second, I define my situation in time and place, whatever it is, and I am defined by it. Third, I am unique: without each ingredient in my situation, I would not be me, whether this ingredient is as small as a single word or as big as a war.

SOCRATES: Thank you for the short and simple summary. But I still do not see how you could say that to the Jew in the death camp. First, you say he is responsible for being in this war, and even for being gassed, because he has chosen not to commit suicide. That sounds as if you make him guilty of either murder or suicide. Hardly a choice! There is no good choice there, no choice between good and evil. Is that what you call your philosophy of *freedom*? Second, you say that he defines *and is defined by* his situation. Is this your autonomous individual? Third, you say he must be without remorse or regret. Would you preach that to Hitler and his henchmen too? That they should be without remorse or regret?

SARTRE: Socrates, I thought you always had the habit of trying to understand a man before you refuted him. Do you really think that you understand what I have written?

SOCRATES: Indeed not! That is why I asked you those questions: I am not engaged in the project of refutation but in the project of understanding.

SARTRE: Why then the sarcasm and the blame?

SOCRATES: I blame you for not making your words clear enough for my pedestrian mind. You couldn't possibly mean what you seem to mean, unless you are morally insane.

SARTRE: I still don't trust you, Socrates. I think this is part of your famous irony, and not serious. You are just trying to turn me inside out and show me up.

SOCRATES: Indeed I am! Because that is what I would want done to me: to have my insides turned out, so to speak—my deepest meanings and my fundamental premises laid bare so that I could know myself better. And I would want myself and my premises to be held up into the clear light of truth so that all my shadows flee. And you must learn to want that too, Jean-Paul, or else. . . .

But that is not my task. I am merely the examiner of your book. And this book I do not yet understand. Will you at least try to make me understand?

SARTRE: Yes. I think you will understand when I explain my concept of human freedom.

SOCRATES: Then let us go there next.

9

Freedom and Values

SOCRATES: I am puzzled by your notion of freedom in *Existentialism and Human Emotions*.

Here are the two statements I find puzzling:

EHE, 45   (1) **Freedom . . . can have no other aim than to want itself; if man has once become aware that . . . he imposes values, he can no longer want but one thing, and that is freedom.**

EHE, 48   (2) **One may choose anything if it is on the grounds of free involvement.**

Do you really mean what these statements seem to mean? They seem to mean something not only shocking but ridiculous.

SARTRE: I can explain them only in light of their foundation, their premise. And that is the premise of the subjectivity of all values. In order to explain my notion of total responsibility, which you find so absurd, I need to explain my notion of radical freedom; and in order to explain my notion of radical freedom, I need to explain my notion of values.

SOCRATES: Explain away, then!

SARTRE: Let me do that by playing Socrates to you for a minute, Socrates. What do *you* think I mean in these two statements?

SOCRATES: I think you mean what you say, until you say otherwise. And what you say about values seems quite clear from two statements. First, **"What art and ethics have in common is that we have creation and invention in both cases."** And the second statement, which seems to be your reason for the first, is this: **"We remind man that there is no lawmaker other than himself."** EHE, 43

EHE, 51

The first statement puts ethics in the same genus as art rather than science: something made rather than discovered, subjective rather than objective, artificial rather than natural. The second statement shows the logical derivation of the first statement from your atheism: since there is no higher lawmaker than man, there can be no higher law than the laws man makes. That seems quite clear to me. Have I got it right?

SARTRE: You do.

SOCRATES: So it all goes back to your atheism.

SARTRE: Indeed it does. And I make that quite clear when I agree with Dostoyevski's thesis that "If God does not exist, everything is permissible."

SOCRATES: And you wrote that you found this conclusion

very distressing because all possibility of finding values in some heaven of ideas disappears along with Him. There can no longer be an EHE, 22

a priori Good since there is no infinite and perfect consciousness to think it. . . . [A]nd as a result man is forlorn.

SARTRE: I wrote that, and I take responsibility for it.

SOCRATES: I want to be sure I am clear about your logic. I mean the relation between premises and conclusions. Is this correct?—you ground your notion of total responsibility in your notion of freedom, your notion of freedom in your notion of values as man-made, and your notion of values as man-made in your notion of atheism. If that is correct, I am still trying to find out whether your atheism in turn is grounded in a still more fundamental premise, such as the problem of evil, or scientific evidence.

SARTRE: No. Atheism is my fundamental choice.

SOCRATES: Is it a *free* choice?

SARTRE: Certainly! It is also a choice *of* freedom.

SOCRATES: All right. Now you say that "distress" and "forlornness" follow from it.

SARTRE: Yes.

SOCRATES: You mean they follow by logical necessity, don't you?—as unavoidable consequences for one who understands atheism as thoroughly as you do?

SARTRE: Yes.

SOCRATES: All right. Now no one *wants* to be distressed and forlorn, do they?

SARTRE: Masochists do.

SOCRATES: Do you think most men are masochists?

SARTRE: Not in the ordinary sense of the word. On the other hand, when we consider the relations between self and others, masochism and sadism are really the only two possibilities, ontologically. . . .

SOCRATES: Let us confine ourselves to the ordinary sense. Are you a masochist in the ordinary sense? Do you find pain pleasurable?

SARTRE: No.

SOCRATES: All right. Then we have a puzzle here.

SARTRE: A psychological puzzle?

SOCRATES: No, a logical puzzle. Don't you see it?

SARTRE: No. What is it?

SOCRATES: That one of three things you say must be false, if I understand you correctly. First, you freely choose atheism, rather than deducing it from prior premises. Second, you know that you cannot avoid distress if you choose atheism. Third, you do not want distress.

SARTRE: So how do you psychoanalyze me, Doctor Fraud?

SOCRATES: It is not my task to psychoanalyze you, to discern your motives, but to explore your logic. But logic tells me something about your motives.

SARTRE: What?

SOCRATES: Well, here are your three propositions. The first is atheism. The second is the causal connection between atheism and distress. The third is distress. Now logic tells me this about your motives for believing these three propositions: it tells me that your motive for embracing the last two propositions is logical necessity, if they necessarily follow from the first, from your atheism, as you say they do. But logic also tells me that there is no logical necessity for embracing the first proposition, your atheism, since you say that it does not follow from any prior premise and that that is your free choice. So it is the motive behind your atheism that is the motive or cause behind your whole philosophy. And we have not yet found that.

SARTRE: I see what you are doing now, Socrates. Under the guise of a professor giving an exam in logic, you are really a hunter seeking to capture my soul. Your strategy is to hem me in, like a hunted beast; to limit and then destroy my freedom, transform my consciousness into a being-in-itself, a logical essence, that appears in the world of *your* consciousness—in short, to put me in Hell. You are indeed my torturer.

SOCRATES: It is not I but the laws of logic that confine you and limit your freedom.

SARTRE: That would be even worse! They cannot change, as you can. They have no remorse or pity.

SOCRATES: Do you deny that $x = x$?

SARTRE: I cannot do that, of course. But I *can* do what Dostoyevski's "Underground Man" did. He could not deny that $2 + 2 = 4$, but he could *hate* the fact that

$2 + 2 = 4$. And so I can hate the laws of logic, and *that* is a fact that is just as true as the laws of logic. To use a Nietzschean expression, the laws of logic are dependent on the will-to-logic, and I can repudiate that will-to-logic. I have that freedom. And if you say that they are based on the divine will rather than the human will, I can repudiate that will too—and I do.

SOCRATES: But what if the laws of logic are not based on anyone's will, but on the unchangeable essence of things, the nature of being, the way everything really is and has to be?

SARTRE: Worse yet! So I repudiate that too, in the name of my freedom!

SOCRATES: Ah, now I see your motive, I think. It is your own freedom.

SARTRE: Of course it is. What of it?

SOCRATES: You are enslaved to your own freedom, or rather to your addiction to it.

SARTRE: You know, surprisingly, I *almost* agree with you. As I wrote, we are "condemned to freedom".

SOCRATES: That is not what I mean. *You* mean that we cannot be free from our being, and freedom is our being, so we cannot be free from our freedom. But I mean that we *can* be free, not from our being, or from the freedom that is inherent in our being, but from our addiction to it.

SARTRE: "Addiction to my own being." What a strange idea! I wonder whether that is what Christians mean by Original Sin? Let me follow up this ridiculous idea: what do you say I must do to be saved from my addiction?

SOCRATES: I think you must first be saved from the illusion that the laws of logic and the laws of being destroy your freedom, or threaten it.

SARTRE: Well, then, according to this ridiculous idea of yours, is there any relation between the laws of logic, or the laws of being, whatever that means, and my freedom?

SOCRATES: Oh, yes. They ground your freedom. They make it possible. They enable your freedom to be, as the finite boundaries of anything enable that thing to be itself: a picture, a symphony, a poem, a sexual identity, or a political position, for example.

SARTRE: But my freedom is not a *thing*, a being-in-itself. Therefore it is not finite.

SOCRATES: But it obviously is! You are not free to be immortal, for instance. So you will just have to redo your hypothesis to conform to the data. You will have to say that being-for-itself is just as finite as being-in-itself, but in a different way.

SARTRE: You say you are trying to liberate me, but you are trying to confine me.

SOCRATES: No, you are already confined, by your addiction, but not yet liberated. I am trying to convince you of the fact of your confinement and of the value of your liberation.

SARTRE: But you are telling me that that which confines me, that which limits me, is that which frees me. That is a logical self-contradiction.

SOCRATES: It is not. Here is a very simple analogy. Suppose you are in a jungle with two and only two paths. Two is the first finitude, the first finite number. You want to get out of this jungle, to be free, to be liberated. One of the two roads leads out, the other does not. So you have one out of two chances at liberty. That is one kind of freedom: liberty, or liberation. One road leads to it, and one does not. So you must choose between them. And this is the other kind of freedom, freedom of choice. Only because there are two paths do you have a free choice between paths. Only because there is a finite number of paths, do you have freedom of choice. So finitude does not remove your freedom but defines it.

But suppose instead that you are in the middle of a desert, where there are no paths, or an unlimited number of paths, and no obstacles to your moving in any direction. There is then no choice for you, and consequently no freedom. And because there are no paths, you will never get out, you will never achieve liberty.

SARTRE: So your point is that freedom and finitude belong together.

SOCRATES: Yes. And that is why a moral law does not impede your freedom, either to choose or to be liberated, but rather enables both freedoms to be.

SARTRE: Ah, but this traditional analysis of yours has it backward.

SOCRATES: Has what backward?

SARTRE: The relation between freedom and moral values. I agree that they are not enemies, or threats to each other. But I reverse the relationship between them. I say that freedom creates values.

SOCRATES: That is what you say, indeed:

EHE, 66

My freedom is the unique foundation of values. And since I am the being by virtue of whom values exist, nothing—absolutely nothing—can justify me in adopting this or that value or scale of values. As the unique basis of the existence of values, I am totally unjustifiable. And my freedom is in anguish at finding that it is the baseless basis of values.

SARTRE: I know what you are going to say to that, Socrates. You will say that both my lack of justification and its consequent anguish can be avoided by adopting your philosophy that values are objective. And you will also argue that only if values are objective can they be taken most seriously, and therefore the value of freedom too can be taken most seriously only if we adopt your philosophy of objective values.

SOCRATES: Since you know so well what I will say to what you say, you must know even better what you will say to what I say. And that is . . . ?

SARTRE: That the fundamental difference between us is about which is absolute, values or freedom. Another way of putting the same question is whether values are objective or subjective, discovered or created. Isn't that so?

SOCRATES: I think it is.

SARTRE: And this, we both agree, is the momentous question, the philosophical question that changes your whole life one way or the other.

SOCRATES: Yes.

SARTRE: And my argument for it is simple: if there is no God, then man is the highest being, and the only one with a will. There is no other lawgiver, therefore no other law.

SOCRATES: That does seem to follow. And so do other corollaries. One of them is that there can never be any real progress. Another is that anything at all may be chosen, that everything is permitted. These two corollaries sound shocking even to most atheists.

SARTRE: I affirm both of those corollaries, however shocking they sound. Many other philosophers—atheists and also some theists—agree with my subjectivism about values, but few are logical enough to embrace those corollaries.

SOCRATES: You are indeed ruthlessly logical.

SARTRE: I will take that as a compliment.

SOCRATES: I mean it as such. I think that these two corollaries do logically follow. Let's just see. Take the first one first. Unlike most atheists, you say, **"We do not believe in progress. Progress means betterment."** Why do you say that? EHE, 44

SARTRE: Because just as you must know the certain in order to judge the probable, since the certain is the standard you are using to judge the degree of probability, so you must know the best in order to judge the better, the Good in order to judge the more or less good.

SOCRATES: That seems logical. In fact, it is so logical that you will probably convince many other moral subjectivists to abandon that premise in order to avoid the logical conclusion that they can no longer believe in progress.

SARTRE: If so, that's their problem, not mine.

SOCRATES: Hmm. . . . You say you are responsible for everything, even a war that others impose upon you by force, but you are *not* responsible for the foreseen effects of your own books on people! How strange! But let us look at the other corollary. It is basically two words: "Why not?" If I am the lawgiver, why not do whatever I want? Thus values are "not serious".

SARTRE: I embrace that corollary too, however shocking it may seem.

SOCRATES: And again I praise you for making the options so clear, for presenting your readers with the two consistent "package deals", so to speak. You have shown, very clearly, that you cannot pick and choose parts from one and parts from the other without being logically inconsistent.

SARTRE: But you blame me for making the particular choice I make: the choice of atheism and freedom and subjectivity.

SOCRATES: I blame you for not yet making clear *why* you make that choice. Or if you did give your reasons, then I blame myself for being too slow to understand them.

SARTRE: Let me try again. Here is an argument you should like, Socrates, because its premise is one that you certainly agree with.

SOCRATES: That is true of *all* effective arguments. That is the whole strategy of argument: to bring someone from a premise he already agrees with to a conclusion that he does not yet agree with, by showing the connection.

SARTRE: Well, the premise of this one is two of the things you value most: logical consistency and honesty.

SOCRATES: Sounds good so far.

SARTRE: Here is what I wrote: **"I maintain that there is dishonesty if I choose to state that certain values exist prior to me; it is self-contradictory for me to want them and at the same time state that they are imposed on me."**   EHE, 45

SOCRATES: Before we explore the argument, that is, the *connection* that you claim exists between your premise and your conclusion, let us explore your premise, the one you said I should accept: that we should be honest.

SARTRE: Do you find anything questionable about that premise?

SOCRATES: No.

SARTRE: Then what's to explore?

SOCRATES: Whether *you* do.

SARTRE: And why do you think I do?

SOCRATES: Because you deny it in the very next
sentence: **"Suppose someone says to me, 'What
if I want to be dishonest?' I'll answer, 'There's no
reason for you not to be. . . .' "**

EHE, 45

SARTRE: So what's your question?

SOCRATES: You say there's no reason not to be dishonest. But in the previous sentence you accused believers in objective values of dishonesty. How can
that for which you say there is no reason—honesty,
or avoiding dishonesty—be itself a reason for believing your philosophy?

SARTRE: Read on and you will find my answer:
**"There is no reason for you not to be, but I'm say-
ing that that's what you are, and that the strictly
coherent attitude is that of honesty."**

EHE, 45

SOCRATES: But how can your argument be "coherent" if its corollary contradicts its own premise? The
premise, the reason for your subjectivism is that objectivism is dishonest and one should be honest, one
should avoid dishonesty. But the consequence of your
subjectivism is that there's no reason to be honest,
and no reason not to be dishonest. And then you
say that honesty is "the strictly coherent attitude"!
Surely there is something very wrong here.

SARTRE: Hmmm. . . . Perhaps I should tighten up the logic of that argument to avoid the apparent self-contradiction. The logical form does seem sloppy.

SOCRATES: Did you ever consider the possibility that it is the content rather than the logical form that is the problem? I mean my question literally, not rhetorically: did you ever consider the possibility that it is your subjectivism that is wrong? It seems to land you in self-contradictions. The very argument with which you accuse objectivism of being self-contradictory, or incoherent, is itself self-contradictory and incoherent.

SARTRE: No, frankly, I never seriously considered abandoning my moral subjectivism. This much is very clear to me, at least: that moral objectivism is self-contradictory.

SOCRATES: If it's so obvious to you, why do you think it is not obvious to most people? Why, in fact, does the exact opposite philosophy, that moral values are objective, seem so obvious to most people if, as you say, it is self-contradictory?

SARTRE: Are you falling back on an appeal to the masses now?

SOCRATES: Not at all. I do not say a thing is true because anyone believes it, whether that someone is Sartre or Socrates or the few or the many, or even all. My question to you is only this: Do you understand the position you reject? Do you see what your opponents see, and then see *more*? Or do you see *less*, do you *not* see what they see?

SARTRE: What we see, what we intuit, what appears obvious to us, is caused by many factors, Socrates. It is not easy to isolate them. I thought you were relying on a logical analysis and accusing me of logical self-contradiction. That is easy to answer, because we all know the rules of logic. But "insights", or what we "see", or "what appears obvious"—this is hard to argue about because it is not common to all. Let's leave aside these "seeings" and confine our arguments to the logic and the phenomenology. And by "phenomenology" I mean not *private* phenomena but public ones, common to all. I like to explore these ordinary concrete cases that appear in everyone's experience.

SOCRATES: Fine. Let us take this concrete case then: your own praise of the French Resistance during World War II. Here were men who risked their lives for a political cause they believed in: freeing France from Hitler's Nazi order. Now there were also other men, Nazis, who risked their lives for the opposite political cause, which they believed with equal passion: imposing Hitler's Nazi order on France. Some of these men were French: for instance, the Anti-Bolshevik Legion. Now in the name of what principle did you choose the first cause rather than the second?

SARTRE: My answer is: In the name of *no* "principle". Principles do not justify choices. Choices justify principles.

SOCRATES: That is what I thought you would say. You realize, of course, that that is not what most people think?

SARTRE: Of course.

SOCRATES: And do you know why I ask you that question?

SARTRE: You are testing whether I understand the philosophy I reject. So next you will ask me *why they think* that choices must be judged by principles. And my answer is. . . .

SOCRATES: No, I do not want to ask about their reasons now, but about yours. Why do *you* think choices are *not* justified by principles?

SARTRE: Because principles do not exist *a priori*. They do not exist until we give them existence by creating them, willing them, choosing them.

SOCRATES: So if someone asks you why you fought for the Left rather than for the Right, all you can say is that that was your choice.

SARTRE: Precisely.

SOCRATES: How then is such a moral or political choice any less arbitrary than a choice between soccer teams, or brands of mustard, or mistresses?

SARTRE: It is no more justifiable than those. But it is far more momentous.

SOCRATES: By "momentous" you mean "serious", don't you?

SARTRE: Yes. And I know what you will say next, Socrates. I already formulated that objection: that **" 'fundamentally, values aren't serious, since you choose them.' My answer to this is that I'm quite vexed that that's the way it is; but if I've discarded**

God the Father, there has to be someone to invent values. You've got to take things as they are."

SOCRATES: So once again it comes back to atheism as your first premise.

SARTRE: That is so.

SOCRATES: Your faith in this first premise seems quite absolute and non-negotiable; in fact, stronger than many theists' faith in theirs. I wonder how that could be—how the *absence* of God can generate as great a fidelity to it in an unbeliever as the *presence* of God generates in a believer. Especially if it "vexes" you, as you say it does.

SARTRE: I'm tough-minded, Socrates. I'm honest. I believe you just have to take things as they are.

SOCRATES: Why? Why be honest? Why take things as they are? Why conform to objective truth? Why not rather untruth, as Nietzsche asked? Why not lies? You seem to treat truth here as a kind of God. If values are the creation of our wills, why can't truth be the creation of our minds? And if so, why obey the idols of your own making?

SARTRE: You asked me that question already, Socrates.

SOCRATES: Yes, I did. And if you had already answered it, I wouldn't be asking it again.

SARTRE: My answer is that there is no answer, but that the opposite position, objectivism, is just as arbitrary and unjustifiable.

SOCRATES: Do you really believe that?

SARTRE: Of course I do. Why do you ask that?

SOCRATES: Because there is an obvious reason and justification for objectivism, and you apparently do not even see it, much less refute it.

SARTRE: And what is this "obvious reason"? What clever metaphysical argument do you have up your sleeve now?

SOCRATES: None at all. It is a phenomenological argument, an argument from ordinary experience.

SARTRE: Really? I wonder whether we mean the same thing by "phenomenology" then.

SOCRATES: As I understand it, the point of phenomenology is to "bracket" controversial metaphysical questions like objective reality versus subjective reality and begin by simply examining yourself and your immediate experience without judgment and categorizing; to be more scientific than philosophers usually are, by first gathering data before forming hypotheses.

SARTRE: That is indeed part of what is meant by phenomenology.

SOCRATES: Then that is what I will do. And I claim that anyone who examines himself honestly and openly and without prejudices, anyone who lets his immediate experience speak to him before interpreting it or evaluating it, anyone who *listens*, will hear a word like "ought" or "duty" or "obligation". We could call it "the first moral word". Surely you must admit that this is part of ordinary human experience.

SARTRE: Of course. But that does not mean it is objectively "there", so to speak. Pleasures, pains, desires, dreams, imaginations, self-deceptive excuses,
and delusions are also parts of experience, but they
are not objective. Whether this "first moral word"
comes *from* us or *to* us is the question phenomenology "brackets", for that is a question of metaphysics,
or theology, or ideology. It is a question of how to
interpret our experience. We want to begin with the
experience itself.

SOCRATES: But this "first moral word"—the feeling
of obligation or duty—is part of the initial experience itself. And so is the fact that it *seems* to come
to us rather than from us, whether it really does or
not. We do not *feel* that we freely create values as we
freely create pictures in the sand. We feel bound by
them, obligated by them.

SARTRE: You are conveniently forgetting an even
more primordial and certain ingredient in our own
immediate experience: we experience our own free
choice.

SOCRATES: Yes, we do. But we do not experience our
own free choice of *values*. We experience our own free
choice to *respond* to them, to obey them or disobey
them.

SARTRE: I disagree. We *do* experience our own choice
of values, our own creation of values. I can choose to
lie on my tax form because I value the sports car I
can buy with the money I get from my lie more than
I value telling the truth, *or* I can choose not to lie

because I value telling the truth more than having a sports car.

SOCRATES: Are we doing phenomenological analysis now, analysis of ordinary experience unmediated by interpretation and ideology?

SARTRE: That is what phenomenology is. And that is what I claim to be doing, and what I hope you are doing too, if you want to respond to me within the horizon of my own method.

SOCRATES: That is exactly what I want to do. But when I do that, when I look at what first appears to my experience when I have to choose between lying on my tax form in order to get the money to buy a sports car, and telling the truth, I do not find that choice to be a choice to *create* a value at all. The two values—telling the truth and enjoying a sports car —are there, as possibilities that my mind considers. Both appeal to me. I choose to say Yes to one and No to the other. But only one of the two is a *moral* value, an obligation, a duty. I experience no obligation to have a sports car. But I do experience an obligation to tell the truth and not to lie. I experience a *desire* to have a sports car, and I may also experience a desire to tell the truth and not to lie; so I choose between these two desires, as I choose between two notes to play on an instrument. But the music tells me which note to play. The music is not another note. The moral law, which seems to *command* me to tell the truth, is not the same *kind* of thing as the pleasure the sports car offers me, or even the pleasure a good conscience offers me. When I make this choice, I do not choose between two pleasures—driving a sports car versus having a good conscience—but between obeying or disobeying what I experience as my duty. At least, that is how I analyze my immediate experience of moral choice. And I think it is also how most people would analyze it, even those who say that this experience of duty does not come from anything other than society, or my super-ego, or something less than an objectively real moral law.

So what I am wondering about now is this: do you *have* the common experience of moral duty or not? If so, where does it appear in your experience and how do you account for it? If not, we cannot argue at all because you simply have no moral data. We are like a sighted man and a blind man arguing about color.

SARTRE: Of course I have the moral experience of duty. But it is not simple and clear and black or white, like yours. That is one difference between us. Another is that I experience myself as *free* in choosing a value, or a set of values, while you do not. So I think we do differ in moral experience itself, and not just in our different interpretations of it.

For instance, to take my first point: I frequently experience the conflict not just of desires but also of moral values. Take my example of the soldier who came to me during the War asking my advice about how to make the choice between fighting for the Resistance or going home to nurse his dying mother. He experienced both as moral goods, and felt a moral obligation to do both, but he couldn't do both at once. So he had to choose between these two moral values. No universal moral sheet music told him which notes to play.

SOCRATES: I see. I do think there are examples like that, where one's duty is *not* clear, though for most people they seem to be the exception while for you they seem to be the rule. But the important thing is that even this poor man first had to experience these two actions as two moral values, as obligations, not just as desires. That's the immediate experience I'm talking about: the experience of being morally obligated, or duty-bound, whether clearly or not. It certainly *feels* as if these values are being "imposed on us" from without, whether they are or not. That's why I say that the *apparent* objectivity of values, at least, is part of the data.

SARTRE: And I say that this is an infantile voice; that in hearing this "first moral voice" we are hearing only an echo of a voice we sent out first, like a yodeler with severe short-term memory deficit, hearing his own echo from a canyon and forgetting that it is the echo of his own voice, and taking it for the voice of God.

SOCRATES: That is one possible interpretation of moral experience. But whether true or false, it is interpretation, not data. Even if it is the true interpretation, we still *seem* to hear the voice of an Other. That is our primary data. And if you do not understand that *that* is why most people believe in moral objectivism, then you do not understand the philosophy you reject.

Worse, if you don't even hear this data, then your moral ear, or conscience, is related to this data as the eye of a color-blind man is related to color. In that case, you have abdicated your right to argue about it at all, no matter how brilliantly you may argue. For you have no data, while most of the rest of humanity has.

So I ask you now: Do you have this data? Do you hear what I have called "the first moral word"? For this "word", for most people, constitutes their immediate and unreflective reason for believing in objective moral values.

SARTRE: I say that they have confused data with interpretation. What you call data—this "hearing" of "the first moral word", this "call" of so-called objective values—I call that interpretation and ideology.

SOCRATES: Then what is the more primary data of which this is an interpretation?

SARTRE: Freedom! Thus I write:

EHE,
46–47

Therefore in the name of this will to freedom, whichfreedom itself implies, I may pass judgment on those who seek to hide from themselves the complete arbitrariness and the complete freedom of their existence. Those who hide their complete freedom from themselves out of a spirit of seriousness or by means of deterministic excuses, I shall call cowards; those who try to show that their existence was necessary, when it is the very contingency of man's appearance on earth, I shall call stinkers. But cowards or stinkers can be judged only from a strictly unbiased point of view.

SOCRATES: I will not take your bait. Stop joking and answer the question.

SARTRE: I was not joking!

SOCRATES: Double bait, then. The man is so subtle that he is joking about whether he is joking!

SARTRE: You can play this child's game forever if you wish, Socrates.

SOCRATES: No I can't. For I can't believe you are serious when you write those words.

SARTRE: Why not?

SOCRATES: Because if you were, you would be so seriously deranged that you would not be here, you would not have any hope, and I would not be your teacher. This is *not* Hell. (At least, not yet.) This is Purgatory. (But only if you want it to be.)

SARTRE: Aha! First joking, then intimidation. You are not nearly as good as Plato made you out to be, Socrates. You are substituting insult for argument. Stop your tricks and evasions and be direct for once, can't you?

SOCRATES: (Astonishing! The man is as shameless as Hitler fulminating against Polish "aggression".) Very well, then, here is my analysis. I shall be as direct as I can be.

First, in this passage you show yourself incredibly snobbish in claiming the right to pass judgment on nearly all of humanity, including all the saints, sages, moralists, and religionists.

Second, you show yourself only half human in showing a brilliant intellect but not the slightest awareness of what the rest of humanity means by a conscience. Apparently, the most basic moral data, the whole *dimension* of human experience we call "moral", has never registered on your data banks.

Third, you show yourself obsessed with your own ideology, for you justify all this and more in the name of your concept of freedom, which is a concept almost no one can believe. For you give to man a freedom that few ever gave even to God.

Fourth, you then show yourself full of contempt by classifying all who disagree with you as either **"cowards"** or **"stinkers"**.

Finally, you show that you are about as far as conceivable from knowing yourself by claiming that this judgment is **"strictly unbiased"**.

My conclusion is that, having lost your conscience and probably your soul, you have also lost your mind.

There: was that direct enough?

SARTRE: I demand to leave this place and this person!

SOCRATES: To whom are you speaking? Are you calling God into existence now so that He can fulfill your demands?

SARTRE: We are going nowhere. You have only pretended to teach, or to enlighten, or even to argue. You just want to flagellate me with right-wing ideological whips, bourgeoise lashes, and Christian cat-o'-nine-tails. We certainly are not arguing. We cannot make one inch of progress here.

SOCRATES: Why should you expect to make progress if, as you said, you do not believe in progress?

SARTRE: And I do not.

SOCRATES: Remind me why, please.

SARTRE: There is no progress because there is no Better; and there is no Better because there is no

Good; and there is no relative good because there is no Absolute Good, nothing for the relative good to be relative to. And there is no Absolute Good because there is no God. And therefore there is no progress. The goal line keeps moving as fast as the runner runs, because the runner creates the goal rather than discovering it.

SOCRATES: Jean-Paul, just one moment after you seemed to me utterly worthless, and almost insane, you suddenly turn out to be utterly priceless, and almost wise.

SARTRE: What do you mean? Is this another trick?

SOCRATES: No, I am serious. You show the logical consequences of your atheism so perfectly that there can be hardly an atheist whom you have not tempted to religion. You must have helped convert thousands.

SARTRE: I am not a theist spy! That was *not* my intention.

SOCRATES: Then it must have been God's intention. He has raised you up to be an unwitting spy, or a prophet, in the ranks of the atheists, to send them screaming in terror into the arms of a priest.

SARTRE: Oh, thank you so much for your words of praise, Socrates!

SOCRATES: But I am still not clear about the one thing I have sought most consistently and repeatedly and assiduously from the beginning of our conversation, and have not clearly found: your first principle. Is it atheism, or is it freedom?

SARTRE: I have already told you. It is both. Either one follows from the other. If freedom, no God. If no God, freedom.

SOCRATES: But which of the two do you prefer to say is your first principle?

SARTRE: Freedom.

SOCRATES: Why?

SARTRE: Because it exists. God doesn't. That's why, right after saying that **"Existentialism is nothing else than an attempt to draw all the consequences of a coherent atheistic position"**, I also say that **"even if God did exist, that would change nothing. There you've got our point of view."**

EHE, 51

EHE, 51

SOCRATES: So all your loud weeping about being "vexed" that God the Father is gone, and therefore all values are arbitrary and unjustifiable—all your moaning about being **"very distressed that God does not exist because all possibility of finding values . . . disappears"**—and all your gnashing of teeth about being "forlorn" when you write that **"God does not exist, and as a result man is forlorn because neither within him nor without does man find anything to cling to"**—all this is a lie, a mask, an act?

EHE, 22

EHE, 22

SARTRE: What an unfair accusation! Why do you say that?

SOCRATES: Because if those quotations are not a lie— if you really do believe what you say when you write that it makes a great difference that God does not exist, then you must *not* believe what you say when you write that it would *not* make any difference even if God did exist. The two statements directly contradict each other. They can't both be true. It can't both make a great difference *and* make no difference. So one of them must be a lie, unless you have severe short-term memory deficit, like your moral yodeler.

SARTRE: There is no contradiction. They are both true. To a theist, or to a theist who has only recently become an atheist, it makes a great difference whether God exists or not. But not to an atheist who is mature in his atheism. It's like Santa Claus. When children are three, and believe in Santa Claus, his existence or non-existence makes a great difference. But to adults, who don't believe any more, it makes no difference at all.

SOCRATES: Would you say there is a great difference between being "vexed", "distressed", and "forlorn" and *not* being "vexed", "distressed", and "forlorn"?

SARTRE: Of course.

SOCRATES: And you said that the non-existence of God makes you "vexed", "distressed", and "forlorn". So the *consequences* of the non-existence of God, at least, if not the non-existence itself, *does* make a great difference to you. So why do you say it does not?

SARTRE: Because it does not!

SOCRATES: It makes no difference to you whether God exists or not?

SARTRE: That is what I said. Perhaps it did when I first realized the truth and the consequences of atheism. But it does not any longer.

SOCRATES: Oh, but I think it does. I think it makes a great difference to you right now. And the difference

I think it makes is this: I think God's non-existence makes you feel exactly the opposite of the way you say it makes you feel. I think it makes you feel not vexed, or distressed, but *comfortable*. I think it is God's existence, not His non-existence, that would make you feel "vexed" and "distressed" and very uncomfortable.

SARTRE: Well, you're wrong about me, Socrates. That is all.

SOCRATES: Am I? Suppose I told you that you had to meet God in five minutes? Would that make no difference to you?

SARTRE: No, because I would not believe you.

SOCRATES: But suppose you *did* meet Him?

SARTRE: I cannot suppose that. I cannot conceive of it.

SOCRATES: Let's see now: you say that God would make no difference to you because God could not possibly be real.

SARTRE: That's right.

SOCRATES: And His existence could not possibly be real because you cannot conceive it.

SARTRE: I said that.

SOCRATES: In order to make that syllogism valid, you must assume that what you cannot conceive cannot be real.

SARTRE: Clever, Socrates. And now you will now accuse me of arrogance, thus implicitly praising, by contrast, your own humility, of which you are very proud.

SOCRATES: No, I will now accuse you of logical self-contradiction. For you say that God cannot exist because you cannot conceive Him, assuming that only what you can conceive is real. Now it is not true of any mere man that only the things he can conceive are real. There are all sorts of things outside our conception that are real. But it *is* true of God that only the things He can conceive are real. So you are assuming that you are God. But if you are God, and you are real, then God is real. So you contradict yourself.

SARTRE: Frankly, your cleverness bores me, Socrates. I simply am not interested in God. I don't want to think about Him. I prefer thinking about real things rather than unreal things. I want to think about man, and human freedom. That is my absolute.

SOCRATES: Then we shall examine your thoughts about that.

10

Freedom

SOCRATES: If you were allowed to say only three things about freedom, what would they be? And how succinct and concrete can you be?

SARTRE: First, that we are "condemned to freedom". In less paradoxical language, our freedom is inalienable because it is given in and with consciousness. We are not free to be either free or unfree; our very being is freedom.

Second, that freedom is by its essence negative: it is the freedom to say No.

Third, that it is absolute, or else it is not at all. It cannot be relative or qualified.

SOCRATES: Admirably succinct!

SARTRE: May I explain the three points by quoting from my description of life in the Resistance?

SOCRATES: Admirably concrete!

SARTRE:

RS,
239–40

We were never more free than during the German occupation. We had lost all our rights, beginning with the right to talk. Every day we were insulted to our faces and had to take

it in silence. [Thus my title, *The Republic of Silence.*] **Under one pretext or another, as workers, Jews, or political prisoners, we were deported *en masse*. Everywhere, on billboards, in the newspapers, on the screen, we encountered the revolting and insipid picture of ourselves that our suppressors wanted us to accept. And because of all this we were free. Because the Nazi venom seeped into our thoughts, every accurate thought was a conquest. Because an all-powerful police tried to force us to hold our tongues, every word took on the value of a declaration of principles. . . . The choice that each of us made of his life was an authentic choice because it was made face to face with death, because it could always have been expressed in these terms: "Rather death than . . ."**

SOCRATES: What a noble and stirring passage!

SARTRE: You sound surprised. Is the idea so unfamiliar to you?

SOCRATES: Oh, not at all. I was surprised to find it in *you*, though. It is a common thought. As one of your poets has said, "Stone walls do not a prison make / Or iron bars a cage."

SARTRE: That was one of England's poets, not one of France's. But I will claim him.

SOCRATES: I am also surprised (or perhaps I am not!) that you so quickly forgot this insight—that freedom is not politically given or politically destroyed—after the war, when you more and more came to identify

freedom with the politics of the Left, and the enemy
of freedom as the politics of the Right. This seems
to be simply the mirror image of the Nazi error of
identifying freedom with the politics of the Right,
and its enemy as the politics of the Left.

But on second thought, this forgetting was not so
hard to explain after all. For we do not easily forget what we ourselves learn by our own experience,
but we do easily forget what we learn only second-
hand, from others. And the heroes of the Resistance
who risked their lives and discovered their freedom in
prisons did not include you. You were *not* an activist
in the Resistance. You did not blow up any bridges or
troop trains. You were not imprisoned, brainwashed,
or tortured. Levy, who *was*, called your work "mere
chitchat around a cup of tea".

SARTRE: I wrote. And writing is a mode of action,
whether in wartime or in peacetime.

SOCRATES: Even if that is so, what did you write about
the war? Not a single sentence on behalf of the Jews.
Much less did you do one deed to help them. You
helped your own career, sitting in cafés while the
real Resistance found their freedom sitting in prisons. Your use of the word "we" in writing in their
name is pure fiction—or pure robbery. Your writing
desk, your basement meetings, were no prison to you.
They were the happiest and most emotionally comfortable environment of your life.

SARTRE: I thought we were here to examine my book,
not my life. The point I make about freedom is true,
however I arrived at it. And I never forgot it even
after the war.

SOCRATES: But you did forget what freedom was *not*. You forgot that it was not political.

SARTRE: And so did you! That abominable orgy of totalitarian metaphysics called the *Republic*—I should call it "the Republic of hypostatized words" rather than "the Republic of Silence".

SOCRATES: That was all Plato's idea, not mine. The god forbade me to go into politics; didn't you read my *Apology*? I, at any rate, never forgot that freedom is not political; that's why I was free and happy even in prison, even as I died at the hands of ignorant and wicked politicians. And that is also why I did not mention freedom once in my defense in the *Apology*.

SARTRE: Because you don't think much of it, do you?

SOCRATES: I think very *highly* of it, but I don't think very *often* of it, because it needs no defense, and cannot be threatened. It is, as you say, inalienable. So I, who hardly ever used the word, was far freer than you, who were always talking about it. As another of your poets has said, "The lady doth protest too much, methinks."

SARTRE: Really, Socrates can't you at least tell the difference between a Frenchman and an Englishman? That was Shakespeare.

SOCRATES: Do you claim him too?

SARTRE: No. I claim the freedom to say No! As the atheist does, but as the religious believer cannot do. As the Resistance fighter did, but as the "good" Nazi cannot do. As Descartes did to all his ideas, for the first time in history, at the very beginning of his philosophy.

SOCRATES: "For the first time in history"? What was I, chopped liver?

SARTRE: He doubted *everything*.

SOCRATES: Not really. His doubt was only a method. And even then, he did not succeed in doubting *everything*. And he quickly ran from his doubt into its opposite: utterly clear and distinct ideas, indubitable certainties, and a quasi-mathematical system in which *everything* is supposedly proved. My doubts, in contrast, lasted a lifetime, and yielded only a very few certainties, which were *not* "clear and distinct ideas" at all, but surprising paradoxes and mysteries. And I paid for my doubts—about the gods, especially— with my life. Unlike both you and Descartes. So I think I know a little about "the freedom to say No" to both opinions and political forces, thank you very much.

SARTRE: Once again I remind you, Socrates, that you said your task was only to explore my book, not my soul.

SOCRATES: Thank you for the reminder. Please excuse me. I may be getting a little forgetful. I've been here for twenty-four centuries, after all.

SARTRE: So what is your question about my philosophy of freedom?

SOCRATES: It is this: If one of two roads is closed, does the traveler at the crossroads have a free choice between roads?

SARTRE: No.

SOCRATES: All right, then let us apply this analogy to a particular choice, for example responding to a marriage proposal. The two roads are Yes and No. If one of them is closed, if one of them is not possible, not in my power, do I then have a free choice?

SARTRE: No.

SOCRATES: No matter which one is closed and which one is open, the Yes or the No?

SARTRE: Either one.

SOCRATES: Now let us replace the particular with the universal. Instead of *this* choice I now ask about choice as such, all choice. If the two roads are Yes and No, and one of them is closed, is there a free choice?

SARTRE: No.

SOCRATES: Then there must be a "freedom to say Yes" as well as a "freedom to say No". And further-more, this must be true both in particular and in general. For instance, if your parents, or your society, tell you that something is true, or command you to obey some command of theirs, you must have the freedom to say Yes as well as the freedom to say No, *as you choose*, otherwise how can you have free choice?

SARTRE: But if that were true of parents and society, it would have to be true of God too. But it is not. For even if there is a God, and God commands me to do something or to believe something, I must have the free will to defy God Himself, otherwise I do not have free will at all.

SOCRATES: Well, of course. Otherwise how could you be held justly responsible for a choice you did not make because you were not able to make it because you lacked the free will to make you able to make it?

SARTRE: Oh. You agree with that. So where do we differ?

SOCRATES: You say that all freedom is negative.

SARTRE: Oh, *that*. I mean ontologically negative. Being-for-itself must refuse to turn itself into being-in-itself, must say No to all being-in-itself. That's general, not particular.

SOCRATES: That's why I specified that freedom had to be the same both in general and in particular. When you say that all freedom is negative in general, you don't mean that all freedom is negative in particular, then?

SARTRE: You may put it that way.

SOCRATES: But you seem to. You say that we compromise our freedom whenever we accept an objective moral law, given *a priori* by God or by nature. You also say that we compromise our freedom when we take marriage vows and mean them, when we will to be bound by them, or by any promise. Or when we choose to act according to any pre-existing roles, whether natural or artificial. Like fatherhood, for example. Or like that waiter in the café. In fact, you go so far as to say that we compromise our freedom whenever we accept a gift!

SARTRE: I did say that. What is your question, Socrates?

SOCRATES: My first question is whether there is a single sane person in the world who has ever believed this philosophy and lived it.

SARTRE: It seems I must play Socrates to Socrates now. Define your terms, please. Tell me what you mean by "sane".

SOCRATES: Would you like a short, simple, direct definition?

SARTRE: Please.

SOCRATES: Wise, good, and happy. How's that?

SARTRE: Well, it's short and simple and direct.

SOCRATES: So why would any wise, good, or happy people ever believe your philosophy?

SARTRE: Are you asking about motives now?

SOCRATES: No, I'm asking for the names of any saints, sages, or smilers who agree with you.

SARTRE: Smilers? You're asking for *smilers*?

SOCRATES: It's a fairly common action. Most people do it now and then. But though I have seen thousands of public photos of you, I have not seen a single one that shows you smiling. The closest you ever come is a grimace.

SARTRE: If life is grim, a grimace is the response of a sage, while a smile is the response of a chucklehead.

SOCRATES: Why?

SARTRE: "Why?" What do you mean, "why?" Evidently you don't understand the meaning of "grim". I mean "totally meaningless, absurd, hopeless, pointless, arbitrary, and unredeemable".

SOCRATES: I understand your premise that life is grim. I just don't understand why you think the conclusion follows that you can never smile.

SARTRE: What? You don't understand why a grimace logically follows from the grim? That's like saying you don't understand why people cry when you hit them.

SOCRATES: Oh, I understand the psychological connection. I just don't understand the logical connection, the necessity. Why not help each other endure the grim? Why not make the best of it rather than the worst? Why double the misery?

SARTRE: Socrates, suppose you learned that your God hated you. Would that put a smile on your face?

SOCRATES: Certainly not. But even if we believe that God hates us, is that a reason to hate each other?

SARTRE: It's worse than that. Since there is no God, and there's no one even to hate us. There's only the universe, and the universe is indifferent to us.

SOCRATES: But even if the universe is indifferent to us, does it follow that we should be indifferent to each other?

SARTRE: I envy your optimism.

SOCRATES: I don't want my optimism envied. I want my question answered.

SARTRE: We are getting distracted from our issue again. The issue was freedom. And I have given you my reasons for my controversial view of freedom, and you have not addressed those reasons yet.

SOCRATES: I will do so now. The question is this: You made three points about freedom: that it is inalienable, negative, and absolute. I understand the first point, and I think you are right. But the other two

I either misunderstand or simply disagree with. So please summarize your reasons for saying that freedom must be negative and absolute. And please do so in the style of *Existentialism and Human Emotions* rather than in the style of *Being and Nothingness*.

SARTRE: Why?

SOCRATES: Because if you do the latter, I fear you will wind up with an audience of one.

SARTRE: I am only talking to an audience of one now, Socrates.

SOCRATES: I was referring to yourself.

SARTRE: Oh. Did you read *Being and Nothingness*?

SOCRATES: Yes. In fact, it was part of my Purgatory, as I am now part of yours.

SARTRE: If I believed in divine providence I would say that it has a delightful sense of justice and irony.

SOCRATES: No, I think you would *not* say that unless you also believed in something else which you do *not* believe in.

SARTRE: What?

SOCRATES: Delight.

SARTRE: Are we here to trade *ripostes* or arguments?

SOCRATES: Arguments.

SARTRE: That was your best *riposte*.

SOCRATES: And that was your best argument. So tell me, why must freedom always be negative, and only negative, always, everywhere, no matter what we do, by its own intrinsic nature?

SARTRE: Because—

SOCRATES: No, no, you can't answer my question.

SARTRE: Not if you keep interrupting me, I can't.

SOCRATES: I mean you can't answer my question because you do not believe that things *have* intrinsic natures. You are a Nominalist. You say that the natures of things, or universal essences, are mere words or mental fictions. How then can freedom really have a universal nature? You deny that man has a nature: **"There is no human nature because there is no God to conceive it."** So if man does not have a nature, how can man's freedom have a nature?

EHE, 15

SARTRE: A merely verbal contradiction, Socrates. Do you want to hear my argument or do you want to argue against it *a priori* even before you hear it, as you have just done?

SOCRATES: Both, I think. And since I have accomplished the one, I would like to do the other too. So I am listening. Why is freedom negative?

SARTRE: Because it is coterminous with consciousness, and consciousness is negative. And consciousness is negative because it is the gap between the subject and the object, between being-for-itself and being-in-itself. Was that succinct enough?

SOCRATES: It was. It remains to be seen, however, whether it is also reasonable. Let us see. You say freedom is coterminous with consciousness, and consciousness is negative. But surely it is only *false* consciousness that is negative? If I am conscious *of you*, then the Sartre in my consciousness must be *the same Sartre* as the Sartre you are. Otherwise, if it is your brother, for example, rather than you that I see, and I mistake him for you, then I am *not* conscious of you, but of him.

SARTRE: Oh, that is a simple misunderstanding to clear up, Socrates. I do not speak of the particular, changing *content* of consciousness, but of the unchanging and inescapable *ontological structure* of it. It is always not-itself, ahead of itself, projecting itself onto what is not-itself, identifying itself with what is not-itself. . . .

SOCRATES: Can't you say that more simply? All that jargon is jarring on these simple old ears.

SARTRE: I shall try to please you, Socrates.

SOCRATES: It's not to please me. It's to cut through misunderstandings. For I think you may be saying the same thing, only in different words, as traditional, common sense philosophers like myself, who am commonsensical most of the time, and Aristotle, who is commonsensical all of the time.

SARTRE: I doubt that very much.

SOCRATES: Well, let's see. We agree, do we not, that I can be conscious of a stone, or a triangle, or a dead lizard, while these things cannot be conscious of me?

SARTRE: Yes. And that is because subjects of consciousness and objects of consciousness have opposite modes of being. That is what I call being-for-itself and being-in-itself. The one cannot ever be the other. If consciousness were a being-in-itself, a thing with a fixed nature that can be defined as an object of consciousness, why then it would not be *consciousness*. It would be a thing like a rock. A rock is a rock, must be a rock, and is not free to be anything but a rock.

SOCRATES: I follow you so far. And I think I agree. We both reject materialism because it fails to explain consciousness. If that is all you mean by consciousness being negative, I think common sense would agree with you too. Only your terminology is uncommon. But then freedom would be negative only in the same way as consciousness: a rock cannot choose to be what it is not, for instance, to be a man, or even to be a bigger rock; but a man can choose to be a bigger man, or a smaller man, something he is not now. He can even choose to want to be that which he cannot ever be, for instance a god or a rock.

SARTRE: Ah, so you do see my point. And I think you agree with it.

SOCRATES: I do. And in my act of seeing your point and agreeing with it, *my* consciousness and freedom were active. But I do not see how they were negative. They were positive in identifying it rather than mis-identifying it, and in choosing it rather than rejecting it.

SARTRE: Oh, if that is all you mean by "positive"—

SOCRATES: And if that is all that you mean by "negative"—

SARTRE: No, that is *not* all I mean by "negative".

SOCRATES: But that *is* all *I* mean by "positive". But I think we should move on to your third claim about freedom, that it is absolute, rather than arguing any more about the words "positive" and "negative". For even though we have left a substantive issue untouched, we will come back to it later when we investigate your philosophy of human relationships. Now I want to explore your idea that receiving a gift limits your freedom.

SARTRE: Fine. But we need to be careful with our words again. When I say freedom is "absolute" I do *not* mean "infinite". I am not confusing man with God. Nor am I saying that *we* are not limited or determined in any way. But insofar as we are determined, we are not free; and insofar as we are not free, we are not determined. The self, the I, the ego, the subject, the being-for-itself, is not partly free and partly determined, but is wholly free. Insofar as we are object, on the other hand, or being-in-itself, we are not at all free but wholly determined. For instance, I may will to live, but you may murder me. My corpse is not free. But my will is.

SOCRATES: That sounds reasonable. If that's all you mean by saying freedom is absolute, you are not radically disagreeing with common sense.

SARTRE: Ah, but I *do* mean something radical, something else than that. I mean that freedom is an absolute *value*, and that means that it is an end in itself rather than a means to some higher end like the Good, or God, or any other thing at all that would relativize freedom.

EHE, 45
Here is what I wrote: **"Freedom . . . can have no other aim than to want itself; if man has once become aware that . . . he imposes values, he can no longer want but one thing, and that is freedom."**

SOCRATES: And this is not what most people believe about freedom, is it?

SARTRE: No. They usually think of freedom as a means to a further end, like the freedom from a barrier on a road that leads to where you want to get to—let's say your home. That would make freedom relative to the end, rather than being the end itself. It would also make freedom "positive", a "freedom-*for*" the end, first of all, and only in the second place would it be negative, freedom-*from* the obstacle only as a means to freedom-*for* the end of getting home.

SOCRATES: I think that is how most people see freedom. Why don't you?

SARTRE: Because I see it as ontological, as inherent in our very being, as being-for-itself. That's what I mean by saying it is inalienable. You see, my second and third points follow from my first: freedom is negative and absolute *because* it is ontologically inalienable. The conventional view sees freedom as something that is given to me or taken from me, as a person removes some barrier or inserts some barrier in my world, like a rock on a road. They see freedom as external, something in the world of being-in-itself.

SOCRATES: Oh, I don't think they do. I think they see it as internal and inalienable and part of our very essence, just as much as you do. In fact, they knew that truth all their lives, the truth you learned only

during the Resistance. That explains your tone of surprise in that uncharacteristically noble passage that
began **"We were never more free than during the**
German occupation." RS, 239

But though most people see freedom as inalienable, I don't think they see it as negative, and they
certainly don't see it as absolute. That's what they
find shocking.

SARTRE: I don't care whether they find my philosophy shocking or not.

SOCRATES: Oh, but I think you do. You care very
much.

SARTRE: What do you mean?

SOCRATES: Like most intellectuals, you are a snob,
and you need to assure yourself of your intellectual
superiority by shocking the masses. If they approved
your ideas, you would only be one of them, whom
you despise.

SARTRE: Once again you are psychoanalyzing rather
than analyzing. I demand to see your credentials, Dr.
Freud!

SOCRATES: My credentials are not that I am Freud,
or a doctor, or a psychoanalyst, but a human being, in
possession of what is ordinarily called common sense.
By the standards of that common sense, when a man
confuses himself with God, or his freedom with God's
freedom, or his relationship to values with that of
God's, it seems the time has come for a little psychoanalysis.

SARTRE: Socrates, we are continually finding ourselves in reversed roles: you are personal, I am impersonal; you are psychological, I am logical; you are suspicious, I am not; I talk about arguments, you talk about motives; I argue *ad rem*, you argue *ad hominem*.

SOCRATES: Role reversal is one of the tricks of my "Socratic method", remember?

SARTRE: Then I shall continue it, and give you a philosophy lesson. Here is my explanation of the difference between my view of freedom, as its own end, and that of the masses, who believe freedom is only a means because they believe in God. Here is the connection: In traditional theology, God wills Himself. He wills only those values He Himself has decreed. No one sets up any values for Him. Now if there is no God, then man assumes that role, occupies that throne.

SOCRATES: I think the God you reject is much more the Aristotelian God than the Christian God. You say "God wills Himself." But in Christian theology, "God is love" and love wills the good of the other.

SARTRE: In that case God needs man to have someone to love.

SOCRATES: Not necessarily, for the Christian God is a Trinity and has otherness within Himself.

SARTRE: Ah, yes, that triply self-contradictory idea.

SOCRATES: And here is another misunderstanding that you seem to have. When you say that "God *decrees* values", you imply Euthyphro's "divine command theory", which I refuted 2,400 years ago. A thing is not good just because God commands it; God commands it because it is good.

SARTRE: If God commands it because it is good, then God conforms to some law, or value, or Platonic Idea of Goodness, some being-in-itself above Himself. Like Zeus.

SOCRATES: Well, no. Not necessarily. The theists say He conforms to His own nature.

SARTRE: I am skeptical of the idea of "nature" or "natures", remember. I am a Nominalist.

SOCRATES: Your confession is noted.

SARTRE: And I am also skeptical of the very idea of God, that impossible synthesis of being-for-itself, complete with consciousness and will, and being-in-itself, with an intelligible nature that can be an *object* of consciousness and will. It is the confusion between existence and essence.

SOCRATES: A theist would say God is the *unity* of existence and essence. Why do you say that unity is impossible?

SARTRE: That is my starting point, just as God is theirs. We do not deduce our first premises from any prior premises.

SOCRATES: So once again everything, even your notion of freedom, which you call your absolute, really follows from the more absolute premise of atheism. So atheism is really your absolute, as God is the theists' absolute. You say freedom is absolute *because man imposes values* — in other words because you ascribe to man the freedom theists ascribe only to God. So again we seem to come back to atheism as your basic premise rather than freedom. Your distinctive view of freedom departs from the conventional one only because man takes the place of God as the giver rather than the receiver of values. God's freedom meets no limits, no objective values to judge it.

SARTRE: And again I reply that my two most basic premises imply each other, and are equally basic: the existence of radical freedom and the nonexistence of God.

11

The Family

SOCRATES: Let us move on to explore your social and political philosophy. Existentialists have the reputation of being individualistic and ignoring society. Do you think that reputation is deserved?

SARTRE: Not at all. Not in my case, anyway.

SOCRATES: Then where do you think that unfair reputation has come from?

SARTRE: It is because people assume that anyone who exalts individual freedom must ignore social responsibility. But that does not follow.

SOCRATES: I quite agree with you that it does not follow, but I do not agree with you that most people would agree with you about that.

But what is the bridge by which you move from the one to the other? For you begin with the individual, don't you? In fact, with the Cartesian starting point "I think, therefore I am." You say outside that all views are only probable, not certain.

SARTRE: Yes. To answer your question about my "bridge", as you call it, let me quote my own words: **"When we say that a man is responsible for himself, we do not only mean that he is responsible** EHE, 16

for his own individuality, but that he is responsible for all men."

SOCRATES: But why? What reason do you give for
this "responsibility to all men"?

EHE, 17 SARTRE: It is this: **"In creating the man that we
want to be, there is not a single one of our acts
which does not at the same time create an image
of man as we think he ought to be."**

SOCRATES: And again I ask you "Why?" Why can't
I say that being a terrorist, or a priest, or a beach-
comber, is good for me but not for all? In fact I think
there is not a single terrorist who wants everyone in
the world to be a terrorist, and the same with the
other examples.

SARTRE: My next sentence answers that question:
EHE, 17 **"To choose to be this or that is to affirm at the
same time the value of what we choose."** You see,
Socrates, it is my very "individualistic" idea that my
choice creates values rather than being judged by
them—this "individualistic idea" is not just *connected*
with social responsibility by some sort of "bridge",
but it is the very *basis* for social responsibility.

SOCRATES: So you claim to base social responsibility
on the very subjectivity of values that others think
excludes or at least weakens social responsibility.

SARTRE: Yes! Precisely because our choices create values, we are totally responsible.

SOCRATES: Like God.

SARTRE: Yes, like God. A very perceptive analogy.

SOCRATES: Thank you, Jean-Paul. Perhaps I will pass your exam after all.

But then your very next phrase seems to undercut all moral responsibility, whether individual or social: **"To choose to be this or that is to affirm at the** EHE, 17 **same time the value of what we choose,** *because we can never choose evil* [emphasis added]. **We always choose the good."**

You make two unusual points here. First, **"to choose to be this or that is to affirm . . . the value of what we choose"**—in other words, choice *creates* values rather than being judged as good or evil by some pre-existing standard of values. That is one point. The other is that **"we can never choose evil."** The connection seems to be that we can never choose evil *because* choice creates value, creates goodness. Have I understood this passage correctly?

SARTRE: Yes.

SOCRATES: So you say that whatever I choose, I affirm the value of it?

SARTRE: Yes.

SOCRATES: And for me that value is good?

SARTRE: Yes.

SOCRATES: And there is no other set of values to judge my act, except those created by other people's acts of choice, which create *their* values?

SARTRE: That is exactly right. There is no God, no divine law, no "natural law", no Platonic Forms, no "objective values".

SOCRATES: So if I choose to be a terrorist or a tyrant —a Hitler, for instance—that is therefore *good*? And if I choose to be a priest, or a saint, or a martyr against the tyrant, that is also good?

SARTRE: Yes. Though I may have to make an exception for the priest. Being a terrorist is much more honest than being a priest.

SOCRATES: I refuse to be distracted by that. I still do not understand the connection, the "bridge", so to speak. *Why* do you say that **"nothing can be good for us without being good for all"** if values are created differently by each individual? I think I understand what you mean by values being wholly subjective, and I also think I understand what you seem to mean by being responsible for others and not only yourself, but I do *not* understand the *connection* between these two ideas. They seem almost contradictory. For instance, being a priest, and a celibate, may be good for the celibate priest, but it could not be good for all, for universal celibacy would mean the end of human life on earth.

EHE, 17

SARTRE: Hmm . . . that's another reason I will have to make an exception about priests.

SOCRATES: What about suicide, then? You would not have any scruples against that, as you would against being a priest, would you?

SARTRE: No.

SOCRATES: Then here is something which according to you could be good for one but not for all, for the same reason that celibacy could not be good for all: if all were to commit suicide, none would be left.

SARTRE: You are *assuming* a pre-existing value, an *a priori* value, Socrates: the survival of the human race —as if that were a good independent of our willing it.

SOCRATES: Oh, please excuse me. I hope you can forgive me for that terrible fault!

SARTRE: Sarcasm is no substitute for logic, Socrates. You know that. I am really quite disappointed with you.

SOCRATES: Oh, lighten up, for goodness' sake! You're almost as humorless as a feminist.

SARTRE: I am serious because I must accuse you, Socrates. I accuse you of being irresponsible in accusing me of social irresponsibility. I was always a political activist, and an agitator.

SOCRATES: So was Hitler. Is that all you mean by social responsibility?

SARTRE: You cannot equate me with Hitler.

SOCRATES: Why not?

SARTRE: Because you cannot equate the Left with the Right. I was always a loyal Leftist.

SOCRATES: Is Leftist ideology your *a priori*, then?

SARTRE: No. I choose it.

SOCRATES: And Hitler chose his opposite ideology.

SARTRE: Yes, and that's all there is to it.

SOCRATES: So Leftist politics is your absolute? Is this a *third* candidate for your absolutely first premise now, in addition to atheism and radical freedom?

SARTRE: No. Leftist politics is our political protection for atheism and radical freedom. Politics is not my absolute. But it is *connected* with it, because the social is always connected with the individual. Sex, religion, and politics are our three most contentious topics, and the subject of most of our jokes. And they are all connected to each other, and they are all part of the "bridge", or the connection, between the individual and the social.

SOCRATES: Well, then, if your politics is relative to your religion—if as you say you are a Leftist in order to protect your atheism—then what about the third thing here, sex? Is that a means, like politics, or an end, like religion?

SARTRE: Both sex and atheism are different ways of expressing freedom. And so is politics.

SOCRATES: Let me see how broadly you define those concepts. Would you call celibacy a sexual option?

SARTRE: Yes. And being a hermit is a political option. And being an atheist is a religious option.

SOCRATES: All right, then. Now you also say that all three questions are closely connected, don't you?

SARTRE: Yes.

SOCRATES: So could you say that sex and politics are part of your religion?

SARTRE: In one sense no, because I have no religion. In another, generic sense yes, for I think they are part of everyone's religion. Why are you asking this? I thought we were supposed to be exploring my view of social responsibility in concrete detail rather than in abstract definitions of these three categories to see how wide their extension is?

SOCRATES: Because I want to understand your philosophical basis for your critique of the family, the institution that nearly everyone else regards as the most essential social institution in the world. But the family is closely connected to religion, and probably to politics too, as well as, obviously, to sex. The concept of "piety" in most ancient cultures designated a single attitude toward both the gods and the family, or the ancestors. And most religions have had a very high view of the family.

SARTRE: In Catholic cultures, that's so.

SOCRATES: No, throughout history. For instance, Jewish, Confucian, Islamic, and ancient Roman cultures, just to name four—the four most stable and lasting cultures in history. Is this not historical fact?

SARTRE: So they lasted long. So what?

SOCRATES: All four were based on religion, and the religion in each case was highly moralistic, believed in an objective, non-negotiable moral law, had many rules and structures for social interaction, and put a very high value on the family. This too is historical fact. Yet these are all things you are highly suspicious and critical of.

SARTRE: They produced dull, dehumanizing, repressive, legalistic, unfree societies.

SOCRATES: Repressive of what?

SARTRE: Of freedom!

SOCRATES: But I thought you held that freedom is inalienable; that it is in our very being and cannot be taken away. If it couldn't be taken away by the Germans, how could it be taken away by the Roman Senate, or the Islamic Shari'ah, or the thousands of Confucian rules, or the Ten Commandments?

SARTRE: It couldn't, and wasn't. But its expression was repressed.

SOCRATES: And if you lived under Mosaic, or Confucian, or Islamic, or Roman law, what expression of your freedom would have been repressed?

SARTRE: Sexual freedom, of course. Moralisms always specialize in that, especially religious moralisms. They limit sex to family, define sex by family, suffocate sex by surrounding it with family. The result is that it is no longer part of the self, part of freedom, part of the being-for-itself of the person. It becomes a part of being-in-itself, an impersonal role. Arranged marriages are one typical expression of this.

Let me quote you a passage from my *Nausea* that explains my "low" view of the average modern bourgeois family, and the average bourgeois man, and the average modern bourgeois virtue.

SOCRATES: Be my guest.

SARTRE: Achille is sitting in a café . . .

SOCRATES: Like you.

SARTRE: Yes, as a matter of fact. I was often accused of spending my life in cafés. One critic summarized my philosophy this way: "Sartre's world is the world seen from the terrace of a café." But this is where I work best.

SOCRATES: Why?

SARTRE: Because a café is the opposite of a bedroom: it is not intimate, not confining, not sticky. No one gets in another's way. All are independent, not dependent; they are free, and indifferent, and objective. I could never work in a home. I could never conceive of myself glued to a wife and children.

SOCRATES: Why not?

SARTRE: Both because of what I see when I look at myself, and also because of what I see when I look at the family. I am one who prefers not to be glued, or gluey; not to flow into and out of someone else. That is my choice. I know some people make the opposite choice. That is their freedom: to give up their freedom. For the family is a glue factory. It is viscous, like body fluids; all breeding and birthing and sweating and spitting and excreting—and mouldering in coffins, surrounded by families with mouldering souls. It is an overplus, superfluous, too much, too pregnant, too *fat*. In a world devoid of meaning, it is best to be *thin*. Do you understand my images?

SOCRATES: I think I do. You speak of the overabundance of beings, including human beings. There are "more things in heaven and earth" than there need to be. In fact all things in the universe are contingent: they did not have to be.

SARTRE: Yes, that's it.

SOCRATES: But when most people realize this fact, it is for them an occasion for rejoicing and thanksgiving. For them, being is a gift. For you it is a pile of maggots, or excrement.

SARTRE: I have used those images.

SOCRATES: So this is the metaphysical reason why you see the very existence of the family, and children, as suspect, as a meaningless overplus, and thus really a minus.

SARTRE: Yes. My point is metaphysical. But I also see a psychological point, a psychological minus, a psychological inauthenticity about the family.

SOCRATES: What is that?

SARTRE: I ask myself: What is a father? And I answer: it is a role. A father is always one who is playing a part, like that waiter in the café. He loses himself in his role. He forges the chains of his bondage with the energy of his freedom.

SOCRATES: A striking paradox! Can you explain it a bit more?

SARTRE: With his being-for-itself, he identifies himself with the being-in-itself of "fatherhood". He strives to become a Platonic Form.

SOCRATES: So it is not just bad fathers, but all fathers; not just perversions of the role but the role itself; not just pharisaical or hypocritical betrayals of fatherhood but fatherhood itself, that is the problem for you.

SARTRE: Yes. And the problem is that it is a role, an *a priori* order, a structure.

SOCRATES: A *logos*.

SARTRE: I have no aversion to words . . .

SOCRATES: Of that we are well aware!

SARTRE: But I have an aversion to the *a priori* word, to "*In the beginning* was the word."

SOCRATES: Is it only *family* order, or is it *all* social order that you see as confining and threatening to your freedom?

SARTRE: All social order is an artifice by which we hide ourselves from ourselves.

SOCRATES: So even this most natural order and structure, the family, is unnatural to you.

SARTRE: It is *bourgeois*!

SOCRATES: You spit out that word with the vehemence of a Marxist! Do you mean by it all middle-class virtues such as family loyalty and marital fidelity —conjugal and filial virtues? Do you see these as not real virtues at all?

SARTRE: Worse than that: the very concept of virtue is a bourgeois concept. Look here, we have let ourselves be distracted again, even though there is nothing and no one here but the two of us. Imagine how a gaggle of little brats would multiply my distractions!

I was going to read to you a passage from *Nausea*. Here it is. I hope you catch the ironies:

N, 19

In their forties they put together their little obstinacies and a few proverbs, they label this "experience" and they turn themselves into penny-in-the-slot machines: the slot on the right is for anecdotes wrapped in silver paper, the slot on the left is for valuable advice which sticks to your teeth like gum.

Here is another passage from the same book. The irony is even more cutting here. The protagonist, Roquentin, is contemplating a painting in the museum in Bouville entitled "A Bachelor's Deathbed":

N,
20–21

Naked to the waist, the torso a little green as befits a corpse, the bachelor lay prone on an untidy bed; the disordered blankets and sheets showed that the agony had been long and painful. . . . This man had lived for himself alone, his punishment—a lonely deathbed—was as severe as it was deserved. This picture was a warning to me to retrace my steps while there was still time . . . among all the hundred and fifty notables whose portraits hung on the walls of the great gallery which I was about to enter, not one of them had died without leaving children and a will; not one of them had died without the last sacraments. On good terms with God and the world on that day as on all the others,

these men had gone to claim the part of eternal life to which they had a right.

SOCRATES: I think I understand your bitterness.

SARTRE: Why Socrates! How unusual for you: your eyes are filling with tears. How shall I interpret this phenomenon? This is a puzzle to me.

SOCRATES: It is no puzzle: I weep because I am troubled.

SARTRE: At the hypocrisy and stupidity of the family that I have just so powerfully evoked?

SOCRATES: No, at something real, not something fictional. I was thinking about your future, and I realized that you would not be able to enjoy Heaven even if you went there: there are far too many children there. I see by your face that you are shocked by that thought. Yes, you would call it a terribly bourgeois place. It would in fact not be Heaven at all to you, but Hell: an obscenely large family, disgustingly happy, full of the very "others" which is your definition of Hell. And there is a second thing that fills me with sadness: the fact that only in Hell would you be able to find what you long for: the purity, the liberating loneliness. You have described the two eternal places brilliantly. You have only one detail wrong: their names.

SARTRE: I never wrote about a real next world, or claimed any knowledge of it.

SOCRATES: Then it is the names of the two earthly roads to these two destinations that you confused.

And that is why we must look more carefully at this confusion of yours, and at these two roads, especially the road to Heaven, which you declared closed. The name of that road is love.

12

Love

SOCRATES: Since to the vast majority of readers this is the single most shocking idea in your whole philosophy, we must try to understand your rejection of love. For one thing, it is obviously closely connected to your rejection of God.

SARTRE: Ethics and ontology naturally go together, after all.

SOCRATES: Your explicit analysis of love is found in *Being and Nothingness* rather than in *Existentialism and Human Emotions.* Nevertheless, we should examine it here, even though we are supposed to be examining only that smaller, more popular book. To greatly simplify, shorten, and summarize an analysis that is far from simple or short, it seems to me that you make four important claims about love:

First, that we all deeply want it and hope it will bring us happiness, or success, or salvation.

Second, that successful love, successful altruistic love, is impossible. Our deep hope is dashed.

Third, that the reason it is impossible is, once again, your ontology of being-in-itself versus being-for-itself. Love is impossible because its ontological structure is self-contradictory.

Finally, as a corollary, you say that our acceptance of love, that is, our acceptance of *altruistic* love, or even our acceptance of *attempts* at altruistic love, in fact even our acceptance of *apparent* attempts at altruistic love, in the form of any kind of *gift*, would compromise our freedom and thus our very being.

SARTRE: That is a fine four-point analysis as far as it goes.

SOCRATES: Then let us explore each point, in order. I must confess, however, that we will be missing something essential if we do this.

SARTRE: What? Add a fifth point if you wish.

SOCRATES: No, it is not another "point", another *object* of consciousness, or being-in-itself, as you would say. It is a certain *mode* of consciousness, of being-for-itself, that we will be missing.

SARTRE: What do you mean? What mode of consciousness?

SOCRATES: We are about to analyze and dissect love as if it were a theorem in geometry or an insect in a laboratory. But what it is, by your own admission, is the *sine qua non* of our own hope of happiness, whether on earth or afterward. So we are inquiring into ourselves, into our own lives, into whether they can bear this weight, or contain this meaning. *Everything* is at stake in this inquiry—most especially the inquirer himself.

That is one half of the paradox. The other half is that we must be objective about this supremely subjective thing, for we must be fair. We must subject love to logic.

SARTRE: We must indeed. I give you credit for seeing that existential paradox, Socrates. Most philosophers did not see it, I think.

SOCRATES: And I give *you* credit for seeing it too, at least in print.

SARTRE: What do you imply by that qualification?

SOCRATES: Frankly, that you often seemed to strike a pose, like an actor. You seemed uncommonly comfortable in your role of afflicting the comfortable but never comforting the afflicted.

SARTRE: There's nothing wrong with telling the truth as you see it with gusto, even though the truth is that there is no ultimate reason for gusto.

SOCRATES: I agree. I do not fault you for your gusto, or for telling what you thought was the truth.

SARTRE: Then what do you fault me for? Will you be wholly frank with me?

SOCRATES: I will. You *loved* your loveless philosophy. Camus never did. He hated it. He was tortured by it. You only played with it, like a toy. *You* could never have invented a tragic character like Dr. Rieux in *The Plague.* For you never agonized over his and Camus' dilemma of whether one can be a saint without God.

SARTRE: Only a theist like yourself would say that, Socrates.

SOCRATES: Not so. Camus said it too.

SARTRE: I was just never very interested in God. Sorry. That's just our bottom line difference.

SOCRATES: I don't think it is. I don't fault you for that so much as for not being interested in being a saint. I think *that's* the bottom line difference: ethics, not metaphysics. You never wanted to be a saint. Camus did. That's a bigger difference than the difference between atheism and theism, I think.

SARTRE: I was a better philosopher than Camus, and much more consistent. He had begun moving more and more toward religion. He was meeting with a Catholic priest regularly for months. If he hadn't died young, he might have sold his soul to the Church, or to the devil—not that there's any difference between those two, really.

SOCRATES: But you at least understood something of his agony, didn't you? You certainly must have felt the existential vacuum at the heart of life that you called "absurdity" and wrote about so powerfully in *Nausea*. How could you write about it if you hadn't experienced it? And therefore you must have felt *something* of the need Camus felt for the thing the saints put into that existential vacuum, namely love.

SARTRE: Are we doing psychoanalysis now, or confession, or philosophy?

SOCRATES: Philosophy.

SARTRE: Then let's stay within what I say in my books.

SOCRATES: That is what we will do, at least for now. In *No Exit*, and also in *Nausea*, your protagonists desperately search for a relationship of fulfilling love, a mutual love that is both honest and respectful, both aware of the other's faults and yet freely choosing to love and affirm the value of the other. You even say somewhere that this love alone could redeem our lives from being absurd, meaninglessness and superfluous.

SARTRE: That is correct.

SOCRATES: But your protagonists always find this impossible. In *No Exit*, for instance, each of the three can *either* love *or* know the other two, but not both at the same time. For you, it seems, these two highest human activities, knowledge and love, work against each other, work in opposite directions.

SARTRE: That is true. But it is not the heart of my critique of human love. You see, my critique is not just a personal pessimism or misanthropy on my part, or a disappointed optimism (which is often the same thing, as if I merely found people inadequate to come up to my expectations). It is a metaphysical analysis of the universal human condition.

SOCRATES: But you say you are a Nominalist, so there are no universals. And you say there is no such thing as human nature.

SARTRE: There is no universal human *nature*, but there *is* a universal human *condition*.

SOCRATES: I'm tempted to ask how that is logically possible, but I'd rather get on with your main point. What is the human condition that makes love impossible?

SARTRE: It is this: We cannot love another in the presence of a third. One subject cannot treat a second as a subject rather than as an object if both are being watched as objects by a third subject. And that is true whether the third subject is man or God. That's the argument of *No Exit*.

SOCRATES: And because love is impossible, life is absurd.

SARTRE: That is *one* of the premises that lead to that conclusion.

SOCRATES: So if love were possible, life would be meaningful.

SARTRE: I have said that, yes.

SOCRATES: But it is not possible.

SARTRE: I have said that too.

SOCRATES: And therefore life is not meaningful.

SARTRE: Why do you go over the argument so tediously?

SOCRATES: To make sure that that was indeed your argument. If so, it is fallacious. "If love is possible, life is meaningful. Love is not possible. Therefore life is not meaningful." That is clearly an example of the fallacy of denying the antecedent.

SARTRE: Oh, when put into that form, perhaps. You tricked me into consenting to that form. The point is not the logical correctness of form. The point is not even argument. The point is the direct insight into life's fundamental absurdity. And that is something I think you have never experienced, or understood, or even entertained the possibility of, Socrates, even though you pretend to praise me for expressing it so well. You said a moment ago you wondered whether I really had as much personal existential agony as Camus; but I wonder whether you ever had any at all. You naïve, happy rationalist, I think you have *no idea* of the problem that love is supposed to solve: the problem of life's absurdity.

SOCRATES: It is true that I have no idea of *your* idea —until you explain it to me. But I thought you did that very well indeed in *Nausea.* I do indeed prefer the rational to the irrational; but I must confess that I find your mouthpiece Roquentin speaking far more persuasively in *Nausea,* without logical analysis or argument, than you yourself do in *Being and Nothingness* with it.

SARTRE: But it is not difficult to put the idea into an argument. It's quite simple, really. The same metaphysical structure that makes God impossible also makes altruistic love impossible: that being-for-itself cannot be being-in-itself. To be a person is to be imperfect, always unfinished, *en passant,* on the way. To be a self is to be selfish. Your religious believer wants to believe in a self without selfishness, an ego without egotism, both in God and in man. But that is simply impossible.

SOCRATES: I thought we went over that argument a while ago. Do you have an answer now, as you did not then, to the simple question: *"Why* is it impossible?" Aren't you arbitrarily erecting these two mutually exclusive categories *a priori* as a barrier against

God and against altruistic love—a kind of spiritual prophylactic?

SARTRE: I stand on my answer and my analysis.

SOCRATES: You stand on nothingness, then. And that seems to be a great existential contradiction.

SARTRE: "Absurdity" is the word I usually use for it. It is the single most fundamental point of my whole philosophy.

SOCRATES: Let us look at the passage that speaks of it most clearly to me. It is from *Nausea*:

N, 76 **All these things — the chestnut trees, the bandstand, the statue . . . abandoned themselves to existence like those tired women who relax into laughter murmuring in a tired voice: "It is good to laugh." I saw that there was no half way between non-existence and this swooning overabundance. If you exist at all, you have to exist to this point: to the point of swelling, of mouldering, of obscenity.**

I found it astonishing that you used the word "obscenity" for existence itself! What all the saints and sages, all the poets and mystics, all the garbage collectors and scrubwomen, throughout the history of the world, saw as a gift and a glory—that things have the chutzpah to say No to nonexistence, the moxie to master nothingness; that they exist even though they do not *have* to exist—this you see as obscenity, as excess, as *excrement*.

And the most absurd and superfluous of all beings, in your vision, is ourselves:

There we were, the whole lot of us, awkward, embarrassed by our own existence, having no reason to be here rather than there; confused, vaguely restless, feeling superfluous to one another. Superfluity was the only relationship I could establish. . . . N, 78

I thought vaguely of doing away with myself, to do away with at least one of these superfluous existences. But my death—my corpse, my blood poured out on this gravel, among these plants, in this smiling garden —would have been superfluous as well. I was superfluous to all eternity. . . .

I knew that I had at last found the clue to my existence, to my nausea, to my life. And indeed, everything I have ever grasped since that moment comes back to this fundamental absurdity.

SARTRE: You have great taste in picking out masterful passages, Socrates.

SOCRATES: And this passage claims that all the wisdom of the ages, all the philosophy, all the religion, all the morality, all the commonsense, is ultimately a cover-up, a way we lie to ourselves about the utter vacuity and emptiness and meaninglessness of existence itself.

SARTRE: Precisely!

SOCRATES: I will say one thing for you: you have dived to the very bottom of the cave, where even suicide is meaningless, where *everything* is meaningless.

SARTRE: Yes. Suicide would only be another way of lying to ourselves, a false hope.

SOCRATES: So existence is absurd. There is no real reason for anything.

SARTRE: Right.

SOCRATES: But if there is no real reason for anything, then there is no reason not to lie to ourselves either.

SARTRE: No reasons except the ones you invent, if you wish.

SOCRATES: And is there any reason for telling the masses, who ignorantly believe that there *are* real reasons, and a real meaning to life, that they are lying to themselves?

SARTRE: No reasons except the ones you invent, if you wish.

SOCRATES: Then why do you write books?

SARTRE: For no reasons but the ones I invent for myself, if I wish.

SOCRATES: So these books are not really for their readers. They are not acts of charity to help them see the truth, to liberate them from lies.

SARTRE: Good God, no! They are not sermons! They are themselves parts of the meaningless excess of existence.

SOCRATES: Parts of the ontological excrement.

SARTRE: You are beginning to catch on to my style of images, Socrates!

SOCRATES: Then why should anyone burrow through your ontological excrement?

SARTRE: For no reasons but the ones they invent for themselves if they wish.

SOCRATES: So you have no reason at all to give them?

SARTRE: None at all. People have strange tastes. I offend them and they pay money for it.

SOCRATES: Is that all you have to say?

SARTRE: Yes. And isn't that fascinating, that the masses are fascinated with that? With meaninglessness, and with nothing, when they say they want meaningful answers instead?

SOCRATES: Do you find that fascination meaningful?

SARTRE: No. I find nothing meaningful.

SOCRATES: Enough, then, of the night. Now I know how desperately the sun is needed. We next need to know why you do not let it rise.

SARTRE: What do you mean by that?

SOCRATES: Your arguments against God and love.

SARTRE: We went over that before.

SOCRATES: Perhaps you could try explaining the argument to me again more simply, in different words. It is hard for an old man to understand such a new idea.

SARTRE: I can do so in *one* word. The word is "I". "I" cannot be "we". "We" is the word of love, the word lovers use, the word lovers claim suddenly turns into a magical word when they become lovers. But that word—the word "we"—is simply meaningless. What it tries to designate is an impossibility. For the subject is always "I", never "we". The other is always other, always object, to me. Lovers talk nonsense when they speak of becoming one without ceasing to be two. That is a piece of hocus-pocus and gobbledegook as absurd as the Christian notion of the One God who is a Trinity. In fact, the idea of love too is a Trinity: lover, beloved, and love as one yet three. The idea is pure muddle, pure mush, pure *m*–.

SOCRATES: What is there in you, I wonder, that is so attracted to obscenities? Oh, well, that is another's department, not mine.

SARTRE: I will lay it out for you without obscenities, if you are squeamish.

SOCRATES: I'm not squeamish. I just find concepts clearer than images, logic a better teacher than rhetoric.

SARTRE: Is there any other way I can pander to your bourgeois tastes, besides avoiding poetic images?

SOCRATES: I also find concrete examples from ordinary experience very useful.

SARTRE: Then here is my analysis, without images or poetry or rhetoric, and by a concrete example.

Here I am, sitting on a bench in the park. Another man sits on another bench. Between us is a tree. I look at the tree and I see it as a thing that lies close to my bench, and over to my right. He looks at the same tree but to him it is a little farther away and to his left. Each of us always acts, and cannot help acting, as the center of all things, the center of the universe, the one absolute to which all things are relative. If I may use an image, I am the sun and the universe is my solar system. Every thing is a planet orbiting around me. I am always at the center. When I turn *so*, you and the whole world behind you are to my right; when I turn *so*, you and the world are to my left. To use another image for the same concept, I am the spider and the universe is my web, and every thing is a fly in it.

The point is that I see that tree as *my* tree. Not that I claim legal ownership over it, but that I see it (and everything else) as relative to the one and only absolute I can have, the one and only absolute I *must* have, namely myself.

And since the tree is *my* tree, it cannot at the same time be *his* tree. He is an alien spider trying to capture my fly, an alien sun entering my solar system and trying to catch my planets with his solar gravity. To him, that tree is not my tree but his tree. Not that he claims to own it either, but *his* consciousness defines it, and places it, and declares its value, its beauty, its meaning. A moment before his consciousness looked at it, *mine* did all those things without rival. Now he is my rival, simply because of the inherent and inescapable uniqueness of consciousness.

SOCRATES: "The inescapable *uniqueness* of consciousness"? But we *all* have consciousness. Surely, it is *not* unique to you, unless you are God and never created anyone else. All humans are conscious, and often they are even conscious of the very same things at once.

SARTRE: But there never actually *exists* any such thing as "consciousness itself", only *my* consciousness or *your* consciousness. And my "I" is not your "I," nor is yours mine. Even if we were identical twins think-ing identical thoughts, we would still be two, not one, and I would not be you subjectively, *at all*, even if ob-jectively we had very much in common, even if we were identical twins. Do you see the simple point? "I" is the only word that is always totally equivocal. We can mean at least somewhat the same thing by any other word, but never by "I". For my *I* is your *you*, not your *I*; and your *I* is not my *I* but my *you*.

SOCRATES: This is true. It is indeed a simple point. But it is not a simple passage from that simple point to your conclusion that existence is absurd.

SARTRE: Existence is absurd because love is impos-sible, and love is impossible because there is no *we*-subject. Watch my simple analysis of the two men in the park closely and you will see.

What happens next in the park? Suppose you are the man on the first bench. First, you noticed the tree. That did not seem too threatening, for after all, was it not *your* tree? But then you noticed the other man noticing the tree, and this alien consciousness was now a threat to you. It was as if a sink had two drain holes instead of one. When there was one all the garbage in the sink emptied out through the hole that is *your* consciousness alone.

So two men sitting in the park enjoying the sight of the same tree are really two rival drain holes in a sink as wide as the universe, and they are competing for every single atom of garbage in the sink.

Now watch as something even worse happens. You look at him, and to you he sits there on that bench of his in the same way as the bench sits on its patch

of ground, the same way the tree stands: *there* a
little to your right. He is another object to you, a
planet orbiting your sun. Yet he is acting like a sun,
a subject, in taking possession of your planets, your
bench, your tree, your cosmos. To him, they orbit *his*
sun.

But then the worst thing of all happens: he turns
his gaze on you. What had been your object now becomes a subject that reduces *you* to an object, his object, just as you reduced him to your object a moment
ago when you looked at him. To him, you are not "I"
but "he". And you are not "here" but "there", just
as the bench and the tree are "there".

But you cannot accept this. *You* are the I, the One,
the God. And there can be only one "I", only one
God, only one absolute, only one sun at the center
of the solar system. Either that God is you, or it is
he. If it is you, then he is your planet; if it is he, then
you are his planet. One of you must lose his self, his
soul, his subjecthood, and his freedom to the other.

SOCRATES: Why can't it be both? Why can't both
become objectified?

SARTRE: They can. Both can lose their freedom. If
one can lose, both can lose.

SOCRATES: Then why can't it be neither? Why can't
both resist becoming objectified? If one can win, why
can't both win?

SARTRE: For the same reason there might be a successful relationship between two masochists but never
between two sadists. Sadists need masochists, as mas-
ters need slaves.

SOCRATES: But why must either be a slave? Why can't both be free?

SARTRE: You wouldn't ask that question if you had understood what I mean by freedom, and why I insist that freedom must be absolute, not relative and qualified; and why freedom must be negative: it must be negative, or resistant, to the attempts by an alien freedom to pin it down, to nail it to the spot, like the sun making shadows. The other freedom and subjectivity, by the very fact of being conscious of mine, reduces mine to his object, turns the living body of my freedom into a corpse.

SOCRATES: So we kill each other by looking at each other, like Medusa.

SARTRE: Precisely. Perhaps that was what the old myth really meant.

SOCRATES: Unconsciously? I thought you didn't believe in the unconscious.

SARTRE: The point is that all men at all times and in all relationships are only able to play God to each other.

SOCRATES: But this God is more like the Devil, or like Dracula.

SARTRE: Hmmm, . . . you know, Socrates, you are acquiring a fluency in inventing images. First "ontological excrement", then God as Dracula—I think my mind is seeping into yours.

SOCRATES: Would that make us a "we"?

SARTRE: Nothing can do the impossible, not even God. But you do see my point, don't you? Each of us cannot help undermining the first and fundamental claim of the other to be the unique center of the universe, the one absolute. Each wants to be God; but there can only be one God; therefore the fundamental word each one of us speaks to every other is the cliché from the old American Western movies: "This here place ain't big enough for the both of us. And I ain't leavin'." In other words, "You can stay in my world only as a corpse, a dead object. The moment I let you be a living subject of consciousness, I become your object, and dead."

SOCRATES: So the only two things that can even approximate love would be sadism and masochism. In a spiritual sense, of course.

SARTRE: Perhaps not even with that qualification, that "of course."

SOCRATES: I see why your analysis makes love impossible. Dracula cannot love.

SARTRE: So you see my point. You agree.

SOCRATES: That love is impossible? No. I see but I do not agree.

SARTRE: Then you do not see. For to see is to agree.

SOCRATES: It is *not*. Seeing is *not* necessarily believing. That cliché is wrong. The act of judgment—agreeing or disagreeing, believing or not believing—is distinct from the act of understanding, or seeing.

SARTRE: But my analysis is logical. Are you now going to complete your betrayal of the real Socrates by preferring sentiment, dream, myth, or wishful thinking to my sober, scientifically logical analysis?

SOCRATES: Exactly the opposite. I see no *logical* need for you to erect those barriers to love. It is *your* analysis that is dreamy and subjective and wishful thinking.

SARTRE: Ridiculous! No one wishes for absurdity. How could that be a dream?

SOCRATES: Because there are not only wish-fulfillment dreams but also fear-fulfillment dreams. Because you can project your own inner darkness and despair out onto the world and cover up its lights, just as much as you can project your own inner hopes out onto the world and cover up its darknesses.

SARTRE: This psychoanalytic game goes nowhere. We are left with opposite suspicions that simply cancel each other out. We are both committing the "genetic fallacy".

SOCRATES: I think you are absolutely right there. So let us get back to the real issue: not each other's personalities but the truth about the human condition universally. My point is simply that your whole analysis, with its categories of being-in-itself and being-for-itself, which makes God, love, and meaning impossible, is *not* the only possible analysis of the data of human experience. Alternative analyses have been available for thousands of years, and they are just as logically consistent as yours, and as consistent with the data.

But no alternative to love has ever been available.

So why not tailor your abstract analysis to the concrete data of love? Why not tailor the theory to the
data? Wouldn't that be more scientific? Isn't it senti-
mental and subjective for *you* to skewer the data just
to justify your theory, which you have chosen *a priori*,
out of your primordial fear of love, or of sentiment,
or of entrapment?

SARTRE: Again you substitute psychoanalysis for philosophical analysis, just as the average bourgeoisie
would do, but not Socrates. You prove yourself more
and more clearly to be a fake. You must show the logical cracks in my edifice. All you've done is to claim
that other edifices, other theories, other philosophies,
have been built on the same ground, the data of our
experience. It is not enough just to note the historical fact that there are other buildings; we must
compare them with mine and choose between them.
Again you have shown that you are a very unconvinc-
ing Socrates-imitator. You have relaxed your stringent
logical demands—or, rather, the demands of philosophy. You would ignore philosophy for the sake of
a happier life. How un-Socratic!

SOCRATES: I never saw philosophy as more important than happiness, which is the consequence of living well. I saw it as a means to that end. For philosophy was not the final end to me. It was only the
love of wisdom. And even wisdom was not the final
end, but only the primary *requirement* for the final
end, which is the Good, or the good life, or living
well. And people cannot live well by your philosophy.
No one who values wisdom, virtue, or happiness
will accept it: neither Christians nor Buddhists nor

Muslims nor agnostics nor humanists, nor even most atheists. Neither progressives nor conservatives, neither capitalists nor communists. Not poets or scientists or farmers or garbage collectors or professors. Well, maybe professors. Some ideas are so absurd that only professors could believe them.

SARTRE: If humanity is so set against me, why was I the most popular philosopher of the twentieth century? I was adored. Millions turned out at my funeral.

SOCRATES: I was speaking of humanity. You are speaking of France.

SARTRE: Well, of course! The French are famous throughout the world for clear, logical thinking. "French clarity" is a cliché, almost a tautology.

SOCRATES: So is "French decadence."

SARTRE: Again we descend to rhetoric, *riposte*, and ad hominem.

SOCRATES: You leaped down. I merely followed you.

SARTRE: Then let us leap back up into logic.

SOCRATES: Nothing would make me happier.

SARTRE: Tell me, then, what *reason* do you think all these other people give for rejecting my philosophy? What wisdom supposedly unites them all against me?

SOCRATES: In one word, the wisdom of *gratitude*. Anyone can see that your philosophy makes life unlivable because it makes gratitude impossible—or, if possible, a weakness, a dishonesty, a compromise of one's integrity and freedom. I am thinking of such passages as this one, from *Being and Nothingness*:

Freedom coincides at its roots with the non-being which is at the heart of man. For a human being, *to be* is to choose himself; nothing comes to him either from without or from within himself that he can receive and accept.

BN, 156

Your great critic Gabriel Marcel said about that sentence: "I do not believe that in the whole history of human thought grace, even in its most secularized forms, has ever been denied with such audacity or such impudence."

Here is another blow from Marcel:

Anybody less capable than Sartre of understanding the significance of receiving or the nature of gift cannot be conceived; it is sufficient to recall his astonishingly distorted analysis of generosity: **"To give is to appropriate by means of destroying and to use this act of destruction as a means of enslaving others."**

BN, 51

In other words, by destroying my ownership of the gift, I put you in my debt and control you, robbing you of your freedom, making you my object, reducing your being-for-itself to a being-in-itself. Is this not what you say?

SARTRE: What I have written, I have written.

SOCRATES: And is this what you mean?

SARTRE: I mean what I say and I say what I mean.

SOCRATES: I find it hard to believe that.

SARTRE: Why?

SOCRATES: Frankly, because I have too much respect for your intelligence to believe that you have made the mistake of the male chauvinist who confuses *receptivity* with *passivity* and passivity with inferiority.

SARTRE: "Sticks and stones will break my bones, but names will never hurt me."

SOCRATES: So you stand by what you say.

SARTRE: I do. I stand by freedom over sheepishness, however shocking the sheep may find it. "I am the master of my fate; I am the captain of my soul." You have still not found a logical chink in my armor.

SOCRATES: For once I find myself at a loss for words. My famous "Socratic method" seems to be impotent. I held it in abeyance for most of our conversation to give you more of a chance to speak for yourself, but I think I have given you quite enough rope to hang yourself. Not that that was my purpose. Quite the opposite: it was to *prevent* that intellectual suicide. But what words of mine could deter your insanity from dancing at the edge of the abyss?

SARTRE: None! For there is no chink in my armor. I have won.

SOCRATES: If that is so, if you have won *that* way, then you have truly lost.

SARTRE: Behold the sheep bleating his paradoxes! There is no chink, Socrates, and that's the bottom line.

SOCRATES: If there is no chink, then that is the bottom indeed. Your only hope is in your chink.

SARTRE: Nonsense. Through every chink seeps water, and undermines the walls of the castle. It may be in the interest of the attacker that there be a chink, but not in the interest of the castle.

SOCRATES: I think you are quite wrong there. For the castle is your life, your self, your heart. And the only whole heart is a broken heart.

SARTRE: That is just your clever, paradoxical rationalization for your failure. You tried to find some crack into which you could insert your wedge, as you did with the other dialog partners whom you cross-examined and reduced to silence after a few blows of your chisel of Socratic questioning. Their armor always cracked, and you administered your *coup de grace*. But you could not do it to me. You can't find that little chink, that incommensurability, and heterogeneity, that anfractuosity, that surd in the equation. And that is my victory.

SOCRATES: If I didn't find it, then that is your defeat as well as mine.

SARTRE: "Your defeat as well as mine"? As if we were allies rather than enemies? Is that what you claim?

SOCRATES: It is.

SARTRE: If you believe that, I have a bridge I'd like to sell you, Socrates. You're just resentful you couldn't find my chink. I know what you would have done with it if you had found it. Confess, Socrates! What weapon would you have inserted into my chink?

SOCRATES: Nothing at all. Certainly nothing of mine. The only reason I wanted to find a chink was to find a place where the tiniest beam of light might enter, and prepare the way for grace.

SARTRE: Grace?

SOCRATES: Yes. For it is not I who administer the *coup de grace*.

SARTRE: What do you think you have administered then?

SOCRATES: Congratulations.

SARTRE: For what?

SOCRATES: For the most perfect depiction of Hell in all of literature.

SARTRE: You mean my play *No Exit*?

SOCRATES: No, not your play, your self. But *No Exit* is profound too; in fact, its most famous line, **"Hell is other people"**, is probably the most profoundly false sentence about Hell that has ever been written.

SARTRE: Are you damning me with faint praise or praising me with faint damn?

SOCRATES: I don't know. For I don't know whether you actually believe what you write.

SARTRE: Are you saying that you suspect I am a liar and a hypocrite?

SOCRATES: Oh, I already know *that*.

SARTRE: Thank you for the compliment. What do you *suspect*, then?

SOCRATES: At the beginning of our conversation I said that I suspected that you are really a Christian spy, an undercover missionary. You have given a powerful argument for religion by showing that a logically consistent atheism is unlivable. And now, having tested my suspicion throughout a long conversation, I am even more convinced.

SARTRE: Atheism is not unlivable. I have lived it.

SOCRATES: Have you? Have you really *lived*? Can a man *live* without gifts, grace, or gratitude?

SARTRE: But *to whom* could one be grateful for existence itself except to God?

SOCRATES: *Quod erat demonstrandum.* I rest my case. You see, I have found your chink after all.

SARTRE: Oh have you, now? Finally? And what is that, pray tell?

SOCRATES: Your embracing of Dostoyevski's dictum "If God does not exist, then everything is permissible." Most people, if they accept this, will conclude that God must exist. For what do they know about God anyway? But they *do* know that not everything could be permissible. So like Dostoyevski, like Ivan Karamazov, you have given them a powerful moral argument for believing in God. You have completed Ivan's philosophy.

SARTRE: I have completed Ivan's philosophy by embracing its consequences, not by fleeing from them, as the bourgeoisie do.

SOCRATES: And that is why I suspect you are a Christian spy. For almost no one will embrace Ivan's principled immoralism, so they will not be converted to atheism but to theism. Only a very few will say, "Yes. Sartre is right. Since God does not exist, everything *is* permissible." They didn't say that when they read Dostoyevski; why should they say that when they read you? Perhaps you gave to the few the atheist's argument for immoralism, but you certainly gave to the many the moralist's argument for theism.

And I think you are a more effective "spy" than most other atheists because your atheism is both logical and existential, both objective and subjective. Your denial of God and meaning is abstract and impersonal, but your denial of love, and grace, and gifts, and gratitude is concrete and personal. It will certainly persuade more readers to give up atheism than to give up love and gratitude. That is why I suspect you are a Christian spy.

SARTRE: But if I were, I couldn't just admit it and blow my cover, now, could I? I mean, suppose Judas Iscariot was really a saint who understood that *someone* had to do the dirtiest deed in history, the betrayal of God Himself, so that mankind could be redeemed. He couldn't blow his cover either, could he?

SOCRATES: If you are indeed a spy and a saint, I apologize for exposing you.

SARTRE: A first for you, Socrates: ending on an apology! And to me, of all people! I think you have never done that before.

SOCRATES: I have never found a philosopher like you before.